Diner Desserts

∨
∨

open

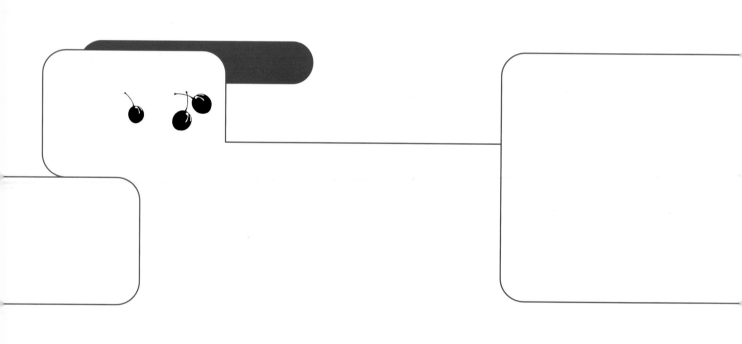

Diner Desserts

by **Tish Boyle**

Photographs by **Clark Irey**

CHRONICLE BOOKS

SAN FRANCISCO

Text copyright © 2000 by Tish Boyle.
Photographs copyright © 2000 by Clark Irey.

Library of Congress Cataloging-in-Publication Data:

Boyle, Tish.
    Diner Desserts / by Tish Boyle;
    photographs by Clark Irey.
        p.   cm.
    Includes bibliographical references
and index.
    ISBN 0-8118-2449-7
    1. Desserts—United States. 2. Diners
(Restaurants)—United States.   I. Title
TX773.B693   2000
641.8'6—dc21
99-38295

Printed in Hong Kong.

Designed by Jeremy G. Stout
Illustrations by Get It Design

The photographer would like to thank all the diner
owners whom he visited. They were very kind and
extremely helpful.

Distributed in Canada by
Raincoast Books
8680 Cambie Street
Vancouver, British Columbia V6P 6M9

10 9 8 7 6 5 4 3 2 1

Chronicle Books
85 Second Street
San Francisco, California 94105

www.chroniclebooks.com

Introduction

I learned some of life's most important lessons in diners. When I was a kid, my father, a doctor, would take me along to local nursing homes to visit some of his older patients. These outings, as you can imagine, did not register high on the fun scale. But my Dad's a smart guy, and he livened things up by taking me out to a diner for a hot fudge sundae on the way home. And so I learned that good deeds were rewarded. Nursing homes took on a more positive spin.

During high school in suburban New Jersey, the Plaza Diner ("where the elite meet," according to the menu) was the big after-school hangout. My friends and I would gossip endlessly over cheesecake, French fries, and soda (occasionally splurging on burgers) and speculate on the personal lives of the waitresses and busboys who passed by. We talked about SAT scores, college plans, and who was dating whom. And it was there, one Saturday night, that a drunken boy tapped on a glass with a fork and professed his love for me before a slack-jawed crowd munching on the Plaza's beloved diner fare. I learned to stay away from drunken boys. At least in public places.

In college, when we got sick of eating tofu lasagna and chicken cacciatore, my friends and I would pile into my fire-engine-red Cutlass Supreme (with a white interior) and head to the Miss Florence Diner in Florence, Massachusetts. Miss Flo's is famous throughout the western part of the state for its outstanding corned beef hash, potato fritters, and homemade pies. It's a real old-style diner, with a bright neon sign in front and jukeboxes at every booth. In my sophomore year I was late taking my last exam before the winter break and was stuck in town for two days before Christmas. Planning to head home early the next morning, I headed over to Miss Flo's for a solitary dinner, full of self-pity. I ordered a cheeseburger and French fries with gravy and played Elvis's "Blue Christmas" on the jukebox. The good food and comfortable atmosphere soon cheered me up, and I ordered apple pie à la mode and programmed the jukebox for a Christmas song by the

Chipmunks. Inexplicably, "Blue Christmas" began to play again. A few of the locals at the counter gave me sympathetic looks. The bouffant-haired waitress approached with my pie and said, "What's with you and the King, hon?" I shrugged and explained that I must have pushed the wrong buttons. The pie was wonderful, and every time I hear "Blue Christmas" I long for a piece and think of Miss Flo's.

Most people in America can recall a diner experience. This modest eatery has become a cultural institution. Although the first diners appeared in New England in the nineteenth century, they have spread from coast to coast, across much of Canada, north to the Alaskan wilderness, and even beyond. The scope of the diner phenomenon can be appreciated by visiting the Internet: a single inquiry turned up over twenty-four thousand items on just one search engine. One of them was *Roadside Magazine,* the unofficial Web site for North American diners. Another was a chamber-of-commerce-type promotion from South Africa's Zulu state, inviting visitors to patronize Porky's Family Diner in Empfanga, the state capital. Of course, diner settings have been a staple on television *(Happy Days,* and *Alice)* and in films for decades. Movies that immediately come to mind are *Five Easy Pieces, American Graffiti, Diner, Frankie and Johnny, Pulp Fiction,* and *Pleasantville,* to name only a few.

Diners evoke a simpler way of life, a time when people ate French fries and cheeseburgers and sundaes without thought of fat, sugar, and cholesterol, when Formica was fashionable and playing records on the jukebox was good entertainment. Diners are warm and inviting, bustling with activity and chatter, with soft music playing and the aroma of strong coffee and freshly baked pie filling the air. They are purely American, and the food is uncomplicated, generously portioned, and inexpensive.

The diner dates back to 1872, when a Providence, Rhode Island, entrepreneur named Walter Scott hitched a horse to a small cart and began selling sandwiches, pies, and hot coffee to hungry night-shift workers. His business was a big success from the start. It was known as the Providence Lunch Counter and was the first portable restaurant in the country. People gathered around the cart, eating their food from the curbside. By the time Scott retired in 1917, the lunch-cart business had become a booming industry in the Northeast and several competitors had emerged.

In 1887, a Worcester, Massachusetts, bartender named Sam Jones improved on Scott's concept by introducing the first sit-down diner. It was a lunch wagon equipped with an eating counter, stools, and a complete kitchen. A huge success, Jones's state-of-the-art operation was widely copied. In 1888, a former lunch-cart counter boy named Thomas Buckley built his first lunch wagon, which he named

The Owl. Buckley began to manufacture standardized models of his Owl wagons and set them up around the country. This gained him the nickname the Lunch Wagon King. His Owl models had built-in stoves that allowed for menus that included hot meals. Diner competition became fierce, and rival businesses popped up in cities across the United States.

As the portable diner business grew, residents began to complain that the lunch wagons were unsightly. In the early 1900s, with this criticism in mind, a New Rochelle manufacturer named Patrick Tierney designed a sleek, prefabricated dining structure with all the amenities. It was a long, narrow building, similar in appearance to a railroad dining car but not mobile. It was called a dining car, which was eventually shortened to diner. Tierney's diners were compact restaurants with gleaming tile floors, shiny metal dining counters, indoor toilets, and separate booths for table service. His design became the model for the diner as we know it today.

The current popularity of the diner is due in part to its friendly atmosphere and spirit of camaraderie. The other, and more important, key to its success is tasty food that is filling, affordable, and quickly prepared. Diners have always served home-style food. On the savory side, menus may include such dishes as chicken-fried steak with a side of hash browns, meat loaf and mashed potatoes with gravy, or macaroni and cheese topped with buttery bread crumbs. While the menu items are all basic, they are rich in flavor and, of course, fat. Desserts follow the same formula. A typical diner menu may include butterscotch pudding, strawberry cheesecake, coconut cream pie, and devil's food cake. These desserts are all lavish in a home-cooked way, and this is the source of their appeal. They tend to be unpretentious, with strong, vibrant flavors and an emphasis on freshness. It is unlikely that a diner menu would include anything that is fussy or time-consuming to prepare. Napoleons, profiteroles, and other staples of haute cuisine found on the menus of highbrow restaurants are not diner fare.

Diner-style desserts are now more popular than ever, symbolizing our love for the plain, unadorned desserts of the past. The recipes in this book are inspired by all the desserts traditionally found on diner menus. They are made fresh every day from primary ingredients. There is no skimping on eggs, butter, or cream. They are oversized, bold, and sincere. Whether what you crave is a piece of cherry pie à la mode, a bowl of luscious chocolate pudding, or a hot fudge sundae, you will find your favorite diner-dessert memory in these pages.

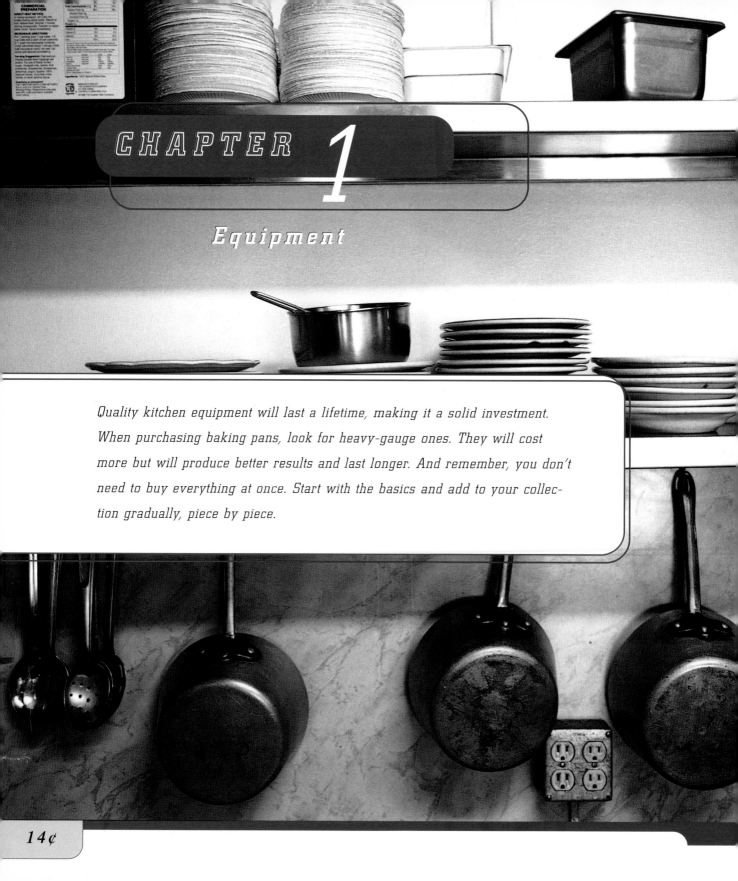

CHAPTER 1

Equipment

Quality kitchen equipment will last a lifetime, making it a solid investment. When purchasing baking pans, look for heavy-gauge ones. They will cost more but will produce better results and last longer. And remember, you don't need to buy everything at once. Start with the basics and add to your collection gradually, piece by piece.

Electric Mixers

While many of the recipes in this book can be made with a handheld electric mixer, a heavy-duty stand mixer is a great convenience. If you bake regularly, you should invest in one. I recommend KitchenAid brand mixers.

$4^1/_2$- or 5-quart electric stand mixer with paddle, whisk, and dough hook attachments

Handheld electric mixer

Food Processor

This appliance is indispensable for many tasks (grinding nuts, making cookie crumbs, mixing pie dough) and saves time chopping ingredients. I recommend Cuisinart brand, which has a variety of models available.

Basic Equipment

Stainless steel dry measuring cups: $^1/_4$, $^1/_3$, $^1/_2$, and 1 cup

Pyrex liquid measuring cups: 8, 16, and 32 ounce

Stainless steel measuring spoons: $^1/_8$, $^1/_4$, $^1/_2$, and 1 teaspoon and 1 tablespoon

Kitchen scale with ounce measurements

Stainless steel mixing bowls: 1, 2, 3, and 4 quart

Large cutting board

Rolling pin

Pastry blender

Citrus zester

Juicer

Fruit corer

Pie weights, dried beans, or rice for blind baking pie crusts

Two pastry brushes

Kitchen timer

Instant-read thermometer

Oven thermometer

Candy thermometer

Two cooling racks

Biscuit cutters: 2, $2^1/_4$, 3, and $3^1/_2$ inch

3-inch doughnut cutter

Fluted pastry wheel

Rubber spatulas in assorted sizes

Heatproof rubber spatula

Small offset metal spatula

Large offset metal spatula

3-inch paring knife

6-inch utility knife

10- or 12-inch chef's knife

Long, serrated knife

Vegetable peeler

Slotted spoon

Cherry pitter

Wooden spoons in assorted sizes

Sifter

Fine-mesh sieve

Wire whisks in assorted sizes

Ice cream scoop

Parchment paper

Toothpicks or cake tester

Pots and Pans

Heavy saucepans: 1, 2, and 3 quart

12-inch frying pan

Deep fryer or 8-quart stockpot

Double boiler

Baking Pans and Equipment

Three 8-inch round cake pans (2 inches high)

Three 9-inch round cake pans (2 inches high)

9-inch glass pie plate

9- or $9^1/_2$-inch deep-dish glass pie plate

7-by-11-by-$1^1/_2$-inch Pyrex glass baking dish

9-by-13-inch glass baking dish

Shallow 2-quart glass baking dish

$10^{1}/_{2}$-by-$15^{1}/_{2}$-by-1-inch jelly roll pan

$11^{1}/_{2}$-by-$17^{1}/_{2}$-by-1-inch shallow baking pan

8-inch square baking pan

9-inch square baking pan

9-by-13-by-$1^{1}/_{2}$-inch baking pan

9- or $9^{1}/_{2}$-inch springform pan

Two standard cookie sheets

Two insulated cookie sheets

Two large baking sheets

12-cup standard (3-ounce) muffin pan

6-cup jumbo (8-ounce) muffin pan

6- and 8-ounce Pyrex custard cups or ovenproof ramekins

Garnishing and Serving Equipment

Cake comb

14- or 16-inch pastry bag

Assorted medium and large plain and star-shaped Ateco pastry tips

Four sundae glasses

Two banana split dishes

Two tall 18-ounce glasses

CHAPTER 2

Ingredients

Real is always better than fake when it comes to buying ingredients for recipes in this book. And quality real is often better than cheap real. Be careful about choosing your supermarket's house label, or other brands with an institutional bent, just to save money. Choose unsalted butter over margarine. Pay extra for pure vanilla extract. Your desserts will taste that much better. Select ripe, fresh fruit. Use baking powder and quality spices that are less than a year old and have been properly stored (preferably in an airtight container in a cool, dry place, and never near the stove). Quality ingredients are essential to delicious desserts, and your time and effort in the kitchen deserve the best.

Flours

Bleached all-purpose flour

This is an enriched pure white flour blend of hard and soft wheat that has undergone a chemical bleaching process that diminishes the strength of the gluten (protein) and thus produces a more tender dough. I recommend this flour, simply called all-purpose flour, for making pie crusts.

Unbleached all-purpose flour

Also made from a blend of hard and soft wheat, this enriched flour is slightly off-white because it has not been chemically bleached. Bleached and unbleached flour can be used interchangeably in recipes.

Cake flour

Made from soft wheat, this flour is very finely milled and usually bleached. It comes in two varieties: plain and self-rising. Always use plain cake flour unless otherwise specified, as self-rising contains baking powder and salt.

Bread flour

A hard-wheat flour used for bread and a few pastries that need a strong network of gluten.

Fats

Butter

Its creaming abilities and flavor make butter the most important fat for baking. It is produced in salted and unsalted forms. Always use unsalted butter in baking, as it permits you to control the salt content of the recipe. Be sure to have butter at the temperature specified in a recipe (softened butter should be at or near room temperature) and never substitute margarine for butter in baking.

Solid vegetable shortening

Because it is 100 percent fat and contains no water or minerals, vegetable shortening works better than butter for making crisp and flaky pastry. Since it is flavorless, it should be used in combination with butter. Stay away from the artificial butter-flavored shortening now available.

Sugars and Other Sweeteners

Granulated sugar

Derived from sugarcane or sugar beets, it should be used when a recipe calls for "sugar."

Superfine sugar

Also known as bar or castor sugar, superfine sugar is very fine grained and dissolves more easily than regular granulated sugar. It can be substituted for granulated sugar in equal amounts in recipes.

Confectioners' sugar

Also called powdered sugar, this is granulated sugar that has been processed to a powder. A small amount of cornstarch has been added to prevent clumping, but it should still be sifted before use. Less sweet than granulated sugar, it cannot be substituted in equal amounts for granulated sugar.

Brown sugar

This is white sugar that has been combined with molasses. There are two types: light and dark. As their respective names imply, light brown sugar has a more delicate flavor and lighter color than its darker, more intensely flavored counterpart. Because it has a tendency to dry out and become rock-hard, brown sugar should be stored in the refrigerator, tightly wrapped in a plastic bag inside an airtight container.

Molasses

A by-product of the sugar refining process, molasses is a thick, brownish-black syrup with a distinct, heavy flavor. It is sold in two forms, sulfured and unsulfured. Sulfured molasses generally has a more pronounced molasses flavor than unsulfured.

Barley malt syrup

Also known as malt extract, this is a natural sweetener made from ground corn and sprouted barley. It has an earthy malt flavor that is more pronounced than malted-milk powder. Look for it in health-food stores.

Honey

Honey is a golden syrup with a slightly higher sweetening power than sugar and a mild but distinct flavor. This flavor varies depending on its flower source. Honey can be used in place of sugar in equal amounts, but because of its water content, reduce the amount of liquid in the recipe by $1/4$ cup for each cup of honey used.

Corn syrup

This thick, sweet syrup is made from cornstarch that has been processed with enzymes or acids. It comes in two types: light and dark. Light corn syrup is crystal clear and has a mild flavor, while dark corn syrup is the color of molasses and has a deep, full flavor.

Maple syrup

To make this rich, amber syrup, the sap of the maple tree is boiled down until it's thick and flavorful. Always use pure maple syrup, not maple-flavored syrup.

Cornstarch

Derived from the corn kernel, this powdery thickening agent is used in this book to thicken puddings and pie fillings. It should always be dissolved in a small amount of cold liquid before being stirred into a hot mixture. Once the mixture is brought to a boil, allow it to boil for a minute. Cornstarch may start to break down if cooked too long or stirred too vigorously.

Leaveners

Baking powder

This leavener is composed of baking soda, cream of tartar, and cornstarch. When combined with a liquid it releases carbon dioxide. Always use double-acting baking powder, the most common type, which releases some carbon dioxide when moistened and more when exposed to oven heat. Baking powder has a shelf life of about a year, after which it loses its strength. To test it, sprinkle some over hot water. If it fizzes, it is still active.

Baking soda

A leavener that produces carbon-dioxide bubbles when combined with an acid such as buttermilk or yogurt. It has an indefinite shelf life if stored in a dry place.

Yeast

This living organism leavens through the process of fermentation. The recipes in this book call for active dry yeast. Do not substitute instant or rapid-rise (quick-rising) dry yeast. Store dry yeast packets in the refrigerator.

Eggs

The recipes in this book were developed using large eggs. Some recipes call for eggs at room temperature. To accelerate this step, place the eggs in a bowl filled with very warm water for about 10 minutes. Always dry the eggs before cracking.

Chocolate

Unsweetened chocolate

Also known as baking chocolate, this chocolate consists of chocolate liquor (ground cocoa nibs) and lecithin (a stabilizer). It does not contain sugar. It should be used when specified, but never as a substitute for semisweet or bittersweet chocolate. I recommend Baker's brand.

Semisweet and bittersweet chocolate

These chocolates are made of chocolate liquor, cocoa butter, sugar, lecithin, and vanilla flavoring. There is no real difference between semisweet and bittersweet chocolates; they can be used interchangeably. I recommend Lindt Excellence brand.

Milk chocolate

This is made from chocolate liquor, cocoa butter, sugar, powdered milk solids, lecithin, and vanilla flavoring. I recommend Lindt brand.

Semisweet chocolate morsels

Used primarily to make cookies and brownies, this chocolate is formulated to tolerate high heat without burning. The morsels maintain their flavor and texture after baking. They cannot be substituted in a recipe calling for a specific chocolate. Semisweet morsels will not melt the same way properly chopped semisweet or bittersweet chocolate will. Nor should a semisweet or bittersweet chocolate be substituted in a recipe calling for morsels.

Cocoa Powder

This powder is the result of a hydraulic press operation in which virtually all of the cocoa butter is separated from the pure chocolate liquor. The cake that results is ground into powder. There are two types of unsweetened cocoa powder: alkalized (also known as Dutch-processed) and non-alkalized. In the case of the former, an alkali is added to the powder during processing to neutralize the astringent qualities of the cocoa beans. This process creates a darker cocoa with less harshness than non-alkalized cocoa. Non-alkalized cocoa powder is lighter in color than alkalized and most brands convey more chocolate flavor. If a particular type is specified, always use it. Instant cocoa mixes for drinks cannot be substituted for baking cocoa.

CHAPTER 3

Recipe Techniques

Beating Egg Whites

For maximum volume, always bring egg whites to room temperature before beating. The bowl and whisk (or beaters) should be completely clean, grease-free, and dry. Begin beating on medium-low speed, adding salt and cream of tartar when the whites are frothy. Gradually increase the speed to medium-high and beat until the desired consistency is reached. Beaten egg whites will have a stronger structure if they are not beaten too rapidly at the beginning.

Flaky Pie Crusts

In the Basic Flaky Pie Crust recipe (page 30), I call for frozen shortening and butter. This is an important step in achieving a flaky crust. When frozen fat is cut by hand into the dry ingredients, it should remain intact and be the size of peas. These pea-sized pieces of fat melt during baking, leaving gaps in the dough that fill with steam and expand, creating many flaky layers. If the fat is soft, it is absorbed by the flour and flaky layers do not form. Overworking the dough causes the fat to melt and break down into tiny particles, making a dense, tough dough.

Measuring

While precise measuring of ingredients is generally not crucial in savory cooking, it is in dessert making. Always measure dry ingredients in cups specifically designed for handling dry measures. Lightly spoon the ingredient into the cup, overfilling it, and then level it off with the straight edge of a knife. If a recipe calls for sifted flour, sift the flour first and then measure it. If a recipe calls for flour, sifted, measure the flour first and then sift it.

Always measure liquids in cups marked with graduated fluid measures. Allow the liquid in the cup to settle on a level countertop, then read the measurement at eye level, adding or reducing the liquid as needed for the correct amount.

Oven Temperatures

The oven is the final frontier to conquer to achieve baking perfection. Oven performances can vary significantly, so ovens should be recalibrated every few years. Use a high-quality calibrated oven thermometer every time you bake to ensure that your oven is working at the proper temperature.

Sifting

Flour, confectioners' sugar, and other ingredients are sifted to remove lumps and aerate them so that they mix easily into batters. But sifting is also a way of minimizing the margin for error in measuring. For example, a cup of loosely packed flour will not weigh the same as a cup of firmly packed flour. After sifting, loosely packed and firmly packed flour will weigh the same.

Softening Butter

Many recipes call for softened butter. To soften butter quickly, unwrap it, place it on a microwave-safe plate, and microwave at 30 percent power for 30 seconds. If the butter is still not soft, continue to microwave at 30 percent power at 15-second intervals until it is the consistency of sour cream. To soften butter slightly, microwave chilled butter for 30 seconds at 30 percent power.

Thickening with Cornstarch

Cornstarch is the most important thickener used in diner desserts. It has twice the thickening power of flour and does not cloud fruit toppings or pie fillings or add a floury taste. Always measure it carefully to avoid overthickening. Generally, cornstarch should be dissolved in a small amount of cold liquid before being whisked into a simmering liquid. It should be boiled for a minute, but no longer, as it may begin to break down.

Toasting Nuts and Coconut

Toasting nuts in the oven releases their natural oils and makes them more flavorful. Spread shelled nuts in a single layer on a baking sheet. For blanched whole almonds, bake in a 350°F oven, shaking the pan two or three times during baking, for 10 to 15 minutes, or until golden. For slivered or sliced blanched almonds, bake in a 325°F oven, shaking the pan once or twice during baking, for 5 to 10 minutes, or until golden. For walnuts and pecans, bake in a 350°F oven, shaking the pan once or twice during baking, for 5 to 10 minutes, or until the nuts are fragrant. Let the toasted nuts cool completely before using.

Spread coconut on a baking sheet in an even layer and bake in a 350°F oven, stirring three or four times during baking, for 6 to 10 minutes, or until golden. Cool completely.

Whipping Cream

Diner desserts are frequently garnished with freshly whipped cream. Perfectly whipped cream will enhance a finished dessert, but overwhipped, grainy cream will ruin it. To whip cream properly, always start with a chilled bowl, beaters, and cream. Begin beating on medium-low speed and gradually increase to medium-high speed. Add sugar and vanilla to the cream as it begins to thicken. Whip the cream just until it forms soft peaks. Overbeaten whipped cream separates into lumps and begins to turn into butter.

CHAPTER 4

Pie Heaven

Sometimes, when I'm really hungry, I daydream about a paradise of pies: I'm in a diner famous for its homemade pies. Hundreds of fruit pies, freshly baked and fragrant, cool on racks behind the lunch counter. Cream and meringue pies, piled high with cloudlike toppings, fill the refrigerated display case. Winged waitresses with beehive hairdos and sensible white shoes flit about. One takes my order: A large piece of each pie, please, and a cup of coffee . . .

Pies made their debut in this country with the arrival of English settlers in the seventeenth century. In Classic Home Desserts, Richard Sax writes, "A wedge of pie in a stoneware dish and a cup of coffee—this was the essential early-American breakfast." Although I've been eating pie for breakfast for years, more common is the person who stops at a diner for a late-morning or afternoon snack of pie and coffee. But pie is still primarily a dessert to be served at the end of a meal.

The secret to a perfect pie is the combination of a flavorful filling and a flaky, light crust. A fruit pie should be made with ripe seasonal fruit, and the filling should be bursting with clear fruit flavor. Cream and meringue pies should have intensely flavored fillings to complement the sweet, abundant toppings, and are best served the same day they are made. The recipes in this chapter give you the foundation for making the perfect diner pie at home, so you can experience your own little piece of pie heaven anytime you want.

Basic Flaky Pie Crust

2¹/₂ cups all-purpose flour

¹/₄ teaspoon salt

6 tablespoons (³/₄ stick) unsalted butter, cut into ¹/₂-inch chunks and frozen

³/₄ cup solid vegetable shortening, frozen

6 to 8 tablespoons ice water

Flaky and light, this is the only pie crust recipe you'll ever need to make the perfect diner pie. If you are only making a single-crust pie, store the remaining disk, wrapped airtight, in the refrigerator for up to 3 days or in the freezer for up to 3 months.

1. *Food processor method:* Place the flour and salt in a food processor and pulse until combined. Scatter the butter pieces and the shortening, in large chunks, over the flour mixture. Pulse the machine on and off until the mixture resembles coarse meal. Add 6 tablespoons of the ice water and process until the mixture just starts to come together. (If the dough seems dry, add the remaining 2 tablespoons water as necessary. Do not allow the dough to form a ball on the blade, or the resulting crust will be tough.) Turn the dough out onto a work surface, divide it in half, and shape each half into a thick disk. Wrap the disks separately in plastic wrap and chill for at least 2 hours.

2. *Hand method:* In a large bowl, stir together the flour and salt. Add the frozen butter pieces and the shortening, in large chunks. Cut the fat into the flour with a pastry blender (in a chopping motion) or 2 knives (in a cutting motion). Some of the fat should be in pea-sized pieces, while the remainder of the mixture should resemble coarse meal. Drizzle 6 tablespoons of the ice water over the mixture. Using a fork, toss the mixture until it is evenly moistened. Add the remaining water as needed until the dough holds together. Knead the dough into a ball, divide it in half, and shape each half into a thick disk. Wrap the disks separately in plastic wrap and chill for at least 2 hours.

3. To roll out the crust, lightly flour a large work surface. Allow the dough to soften at room temperature just until it is pliable (about 20 minutes). Place 1 disk on the floured surface and sprinkle some flour over it. Roll the dough from the center out in every direction, flouring the work surface as necessary to prevent sticking. You want a round about $1/8$ inch thick or slightly thinner, and about 3 inches greater in diameter than the pie plate you are using.

4. Transfer the round to the pie plate by rolling it loosely around the rolling pin and then unrolling it carefully over the plate. Press the dough first into the bottom of the plate and then against the sides. Patch any holes or cracks with dough scraps. Trim the edges of the dough with scissors, leaving about a $3/4$-inch overhang.

For a single-crust pie

Tuck the overhanging dough underneath itself, pressing it onto the rim of the plate. Flute the edge by pinching the dough from the outside in a V shape with your thumb and index finger while poking the center of the shape with the index finger of your other hand from the inside.

For a partially baked pie crust

Preheat the oven to 400°F. Line the pie crust with a large sheet of lightly buttered aluminum foil, buttered side down, covering the edge of the crust so that it doesn't get too brown. Fill the lined crust with pie weights, dried beans, or raw rice. Bake the pie crust for 15 minutes. Remove the weights and foil. Prick the bottom of the crust well with a fork and bake the crust for another 7 minutes, or until the edges are just beginning to turn golden, but the crust is not fully baked. Cool the pie crust on a wire rack.

RECIPE CONTINUES >>

For a fully baked pie crust

Follow the directions for a partially baked crust, but after removing the weights and foil, bake the crust for an additional 12 to 14 minutes, or until the crust is golden and baked through. Cool the pie crust on a wire rack.

For a double-crust pie

Leave the dough overhanging the rim of the pie plate. Roll out the second disk in the same manner and place it on a baking sheet. Chill the crust for at least 30 minutes or up to 24 hours.

Fill the bottom pie crust. Drape the top crust over the filling and trim it to allow a $^3/_4$-inch overhang. Press the edges of the two crusts together to seal them. Tuck the dough underneath itself, pressing it onto the rim of the plate. Flute the edge, following the directions for a single-crust pie.

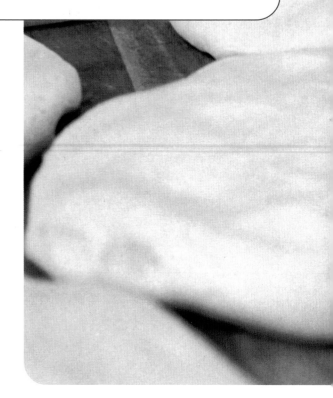

Classic Lattice-Top Cherry Pie

CRUST

Basic Flaky Pie Crust (page 30)

CHERRY FILLING

5 cups fresh sour cherries, pitted, or slightly thawed frozen pitted cherries

$1/2$ teaspoon almond extract

$1^1/4$ cups plus 1 tablespoon granulated sugar

2 tablespoons all-purpose flour

$1/4$ teaspoon ground cinnamon

Pinch of salt

2 tablespoons chilled unsalted butter, cut into bits

A classic diner-style cherry pie combines a perfectly balanced sweet-tart ruby filling with a flaky lattice crust. Fresh Michigan sour cherries, available mid-July to early August, are the best choice for this pie. Frozen sour cherries are almost as delicious, while the canned variety is a distant third choice (see note). The tart flavor of fresh sour cherries needs little embellishment and ice-cold milk or hot coffee provides an ideal accompaniment. Of course, adding a scoop of vanilla ice cream on the side does not detract from the taste of this pie either. A cherry pitter, available in gourmet kitchen stores, is a useful accessory for removing pits.

1. Make the pie crust pastry as directed and chill for at least 2 hours.

2. To make the filling, line a baking sheet with waxed paper and set aside. In a large bowl, combine the cherries and the almond extract.

3. In a small bowl, combine $1^1/4$ cups of the sugar, the flour, cinnamon, and salt. Add to the cherries and toss to combine. Set aside.

4. Line a 9-inch pie plate with half of the dough as directed. Refrigerate the bottom crust while preparing the lattice top.

5. Invert a jelly-roll plate on a work surface. Cut a sheet of parchment paper to fit the pan bottom precisely and place it on the plate. Roll the remaining dough disk into a 12-inch square. Using a fluted pastry cutter or a knife, cut the dough into twenty-four $1/2$-inch-wide strips. Place 12 of the strips, $1/4$ inch apart, on the parchment-lined plate. Turn the pastry strips so they are positioned vertically to you. Fold

every other strip of dough in half, toward you. Place one of the reserved strips of dough horizontally across the unfolded strips. Now unfold the strips back to their original position and fold back the alternating strips. Place another strip of dough across and continue this process until you have placed 6 horizontal strips. Turn the plate 180 degrees and repeat the process. Refrigerate the lattice top for 20 minutes. Preheat the oven to 425°F.

6. Pile the cherry mixture into the pie crust. Dot the filling with the butter. Moisten the rim of the bottom crust with water. Gently force the chilled lattice top onto the pie, pulling the parchment paper and plate toward you while pushing the lattice top onto the pie with your other hand. Crimp the edges and sprinkle the top of the pie with the remaining 1 tablespoon sugar. Bake the pie for 10 minutes; reduce the temperature to 350°F and bake for 35 to 40 minutes longer, or until the crust is golden brown and the filling is bubbling. Transfer to a wire rack to cool. Serve slightly warm for the best flavor.

Note: If canned sour cherries are your only option, drain them, reserving the juice, before measuring the 5 cups and mixing them with the almond extract. Reduce the sugar to $^1/_3$ cup, and add $^2/_3$ cup of the reserved juice to the sugar mixture.

Apple Pie with Cheddar Cheese Crust

CHEDDAR CHEESE CRUST

2$\frac{1}{2}$ cups all-purpose flour

2 teaspoons granulated sugar

$\frac{1}{4}$ teaspoon salt

6 tablespoons ($\frac{3}{4}$ stick) unsalted butter, cut into $\frac{1}{2}$-inch chunks and frozen

$\frac{3}{4}$ cup solid vegetable shortening, frozen

1 cup grated extra-sharp Cheddar cheese

6 to 8 tablespoons ice water

INGREDIENTS CONTINUE >>

The recipe for apple pie was originally brought to this country from England sometime in the seventeenth century. An abundance of apples and love for the pie has made it an American classic. In New England, many diners serve a piece of apple pie topped with a slice of Cheddar cheese. My recipe includes grated Cheddar cheese in the crust: a subtle addition that lends a slightly sharp contrast to the sweetness of the apples.

1. *Food processor method for making the Cheddar cheese crust:* Place the flour, sugar, and salt in a food processor and pulse until combined. Scatter the butter pieces, the shortening, in large chunks, and the grated cheese over the flour mixture. Pulse the machine on and off until the mixture resembles coarse meal. Add 6 tablespoons of the ice water and process until the mixture just starts to come together. (If the dough seems dry, add the remaining 2 tablespoons water as necessary. Do not allow the dough to form a ball on the blade or the resulting crust will be tough.) Turn the dough out onto a work surface, divide it in half, and shape each half into a thick disk. Wrap the disks separately in plastic wrap and chill for 2 hours. (At this point, the dough may be refrigerated for up to 3 days or frozen for up to 3 months.)

2. *Hand method for Cheddar cheese crust:* In a large bowl, stir together the flour, sugar, and salt. Add the frozen butter pieces, the shortening, in large chunks, and the Cheddar cheese. Cut the fat into the flour with a pastry blender (in a chopping motion) or 2 knives (in a cutting motion). Some of the fat should be in pea-sized pieces, while the remainder of the mixture should resemble coarse meal. Drizzle 6 tablespoons of the ice water over the mixture. Using a fork,

toss the mixture until it is evenly moistened. Add the remaining water as needed until the dough holds together. Knead the dough into a ball, divide it in half, and shape each half into a thick disk. Wrap the disks separately in plastic wrap and chill for at least 2 hours. (At this point, the dough may be refrigerated for up to 3 days or frozen for up to 3 months.)

3. To roll out the crust, lightly flour a large work surface. Allow the dough to soften at room temperature just until it is pliable (about 20 minutes). Place 1 disk on the floured surface and sprinkle some flour over it. Roll the dough from the center out in every direction, flouring the work surface as necessary to prevent sticking. You want a round about $\frac{1}{8}$ inch thick and 12 inches in diameter.

4. Roll the round loosely around the rolling pin and then carefully unroll it over a 9-inch deep-dish pie plate, pressing the dough into the bottom and against the sides. Trim the edge, leaving a $\frac{3}{4}$-inch overhang. Roll out the remaining disk on a piece of waxed paper into a round $\frac{1}{8}$ inch thick and transfer it, on the paper, to a baking sheet. Refrigerate both crusts while preparing the filling.

5. Preheat the oven to 375°F. To make the apple filling, in a large bowl, toss the apple slices with the lemon juice. In a small bowl, stir together the cornstarch, granulated sugar, brown sugar, lemon zest, cinnamon, nutmeg, salt, and ground cloves. Sprinkle the cornstarch mixture over the apple slices and toss well to combine. Spoon the filling into the pastry-lined pie plate. Dot the filling with the butter.

6. Flip the top crust over the filled pie crust. Peel off the waxed paper. Trim the top crust to allow a $\frac{3}{4}$-inch overhang. Press the edges of the crusts together to seal them. Tuck the dough underneath itself, pressing it onto the rim of the plate. Flute the edge decoratively. Using a sharp paring knife, cut five 1-inch-long slits in the top crust to allow steam to escape.

7. Brush the milk over the top crust and sprinkle it with the sugar. Bake for 60 minutes, or until the crust is golden brown. Cool on a wire rack.

APPLE FILLING

$1\frac{1}{2}$ pounds Golden Delicious, Fuji, or Cortland apples (about 4 medium), peeled, cored, and sliced $\frac{1}{4}$ inch thick

1 pound Granny Smith apples (about 3 medium), peeled, cored, and sliced $\frac{1}{4}$ inch thick

1 tablespoon fresh lemon juice

$2\frac{1}{2}$ tablespoons cornstarch

$\frac{1}{3}$ cup granulated sugar

$\frac{2}{3}$ cup firmly packed light brown sugar

1 teaspoon grated lemon zest

1 teaspoon ground cinnamon

$\frac{1}{2}$ teaspoon freshly grated nutmeg

$\frac{1}{2}$ teaspoon salt

$\frac{1}{4}$ teaspoon ground cloves

1 tablespoon chilled unsalted butter, cut into bits

TOPPING

1 tablespoon whole milk, for glazing the crust

1 teaspoon granulated sugar

Chocolate Cream Pie

CHOCOLATE WAFER CRUST

Vegetable oil, for brushing pie plate

1³/₄ cups chocolate wafer crumbs

1 tablespoon granulated sugar

7 tablespoons unsalted butter, melted

CHOCOLATE PUDDING LAYER

3 tablespoons cornstarch

1 tablespoon unsweetened non-alkalized cocoa powder

¹/₄ teaspoon salt

1 cup half-and-half

1¹/₄ cups whole milk

1 cup granulated sugar

4 ounces unsweetened chocolate, chopped

2 tablespoons unsalted butter

1 teaspoon vanilla extract

WHIPPED CREAM TOPPING

2 cups heavy cream

2 tablespoons granulated sugar

1 teaspoon vanilla extract

This dessert can vary wildly from diner to diner. Some versions are topped with meringue, others with whipped cream. Some have a light mousselike filling, others have a darker pudding filling. This is my favorite: a rich, chocolaty pudding in a crumbly chocolate-cookie crust, topped with mounds and mounds of sweet whipped cream.

1. To make the chocolate wafer crust, preheat the oven to 350°F. Lightly oil a 9-inch deep-dish pie plate. In a medium bowl, combine the wafer crumbs, sugar, and melted butter. Transfer 1 tablespoon of the crumb mixture to a small cup and set aside to garnish the pie. Scrape the remaining crumb mixture into the prepared pie plate and, using your fingers, press it evenly onto the bottom and up the sides of the plate. Bake the crust for 8 minutes, or until set. Cool on a wire rack.

2. To make the chocolate pudding layer, in a medium bowl, sift together the cornstarch, cocoa powder, and salt. Whisk in about 2 tablespoons of the half-and-half until it is a smooth paste. Whisk in the remaining half-and-half; set aside.

3. In a medium saucepan, combine the milk, sugar, and chocolate. Place over medium heat and cook, stirring constantly with a whisk, until the chocolate is completely melted. Remove the pan from the heat and whisk about ¹/₂ cup of the hot chocolate mixture into the half-and-half mixture. Whisk this mixture into the remaining chocolate mixture in the saucepan. Return the pan to the heat and cook over medium-high heat, whisking constantly. When the mixture

begins to bubble, continue to cook, whisking constantly, for 1 minute. Remove the pan from the heat and whisk in the butter and then the vanilla. Scrape the pudding into the cooled pie shell. Cover and refrigerate the pie until thoroughly chilled, at least 4 hours.

4. To make the whipped cream topping, in an electric mixer, using the whisk attachment or beaters, beat the cream on medium-low speed for 30 seconds. Increase the speed to medium-high and add the sugar and vanilla. Beat until the cream forms soft peaks.

5. Scrape the whipped cream over the chilled pie and, using a rubber spatula, sweep it into dramatic swirls. Sprinkle the reserved wafer crumbs over the cream. Serve immediately or refrigerate until ready to serve.

Coconut Dream Pie

Makes 8 servings

CRUST
Basic Flaky Pie Crust (page 30)

COCONUT FILLING
$^2/_3$ cup granulated sugar

$^1/_4$ cup cornstarch

$^1/_4$ teaspoon salt

1 cup coconut milk (not cream of coconut)

$1^1/_2$ cups whole milk

4 large egg yolks

3 tablespoons unsalted butter, cut into tablespoons

2 teaspoons vanilla extract

$1^1/_2$ cups sweetened shredded dried coconut, toasted (page 26)

WHIPPED CREAM TOPPING
$1^1/_2$ cups heavy cream

2 tablespoons confectioners' sugar

1 teaspoon vanilla extract

Freshly grated nutmeg, for garnish

Here's the coconut cream pie you've always longed for but don't always get, particularly at second-rate diners. Who hasn't experienced the joy of anticipation when ordering a slice of coconut cream pie at a neighborhood diner? Unfortunately, too often what is served is a pasty pudding topped with petrified shredded coconut and nondairy "cream." Blech. This recipe will restore your faith and lead you to conclude that the perfect coconut cream pie does exist. The secret ingredient is coconut milk, which is now available in many supermarkets.

1. Make the pie crust pastry as directed and use half of it to line a 9-inch deep-dish pie plate. (Store the remaining disk for another use.) Fully bake the pie crust and let cool completely on a wire rack.

2. To make the coconut filling, in a medium saucepan, stir together the sugar, cornstarch, and salt until well combined. Gradually whisk in $^1/_4$ cup of the coconut milk to form a smooth paste. Whisk in the remaining coconut milk and the whole milk. Place over medium heat and bring to a slow boil, whisking constantly. Remove the pan from the heat.

3. In a medium bowl, whisk the egg yolks until smooth. Whisk about $^1/_2$ cup of the hot coconut mixture into the yolks, then return the yolk mixture to the saucepan. Raise the heat to medium-high and bring to a boil, whisking constantly. Continue to boil, whisking constantly, for 1 minute, or until very thick. Remove from the heat, scrape the bottom of the pan with a spatula, and whisk until smooth. Whisk in the butter pieces until melted. Whisk in the vanilla and $1^1/_4$ cups of the toasted coconut (reserve the remaining $^1/_4$ cup toasted

40

CHAPTER 4: *PIE HEAVEN*

coconut for garnish). Spoon the warm filling into the pie crust and press a piece of plastic wrap directly on its surface. Refrigerate the pie for at least 4 hours, or until thoroughly chilled.

4. To make the whipped cream topping, in an electric mixer, using the whisk attachment or beaters, beat the cream on medium-low speed for 30 seconds. Increase the speed to medium-high and add the confectioners' sugar and vanilla. Beat until the cream forms soft peaks.

5. Remove the plastic wrap. Scrape the whipped cream over the chilled pie and, using a rubber spatula, sweep it into dramatic swirls. Sprinkle with the nutmeg and the reserved toasted coconut. Serve immediately or refrigerate until ready to serve.

Sky-High Lemon Meringue Pie

CRUST

Basic Flaky Pie Crust (page 30)

LEMON FILLING

$1^1/_2$ cups granulated sugar

6 tablespoons cornstarch

$^1/_4$ teaspoon salt

$1^1/_2$ cups water

5 large egg yolks (save egg whites for meringue)

2 teaspoons grated lemon zest

$^1/_2$ cup fresh lemon juice

3 tablespoons unsalted butter, cut into tablespoons

$^1/_2$ teaspoon vanilla extract

MERINGUE TOPPING

4 teaspoons cornstarch

$^1/_3$ cup water

1 teaspoon vanilla extract

5 large egg whites

Pinch of salt

$^1/_2$ teaspoon cream of tartar

$^1/_2$ cup superfine sugar

During my husband's college days, he frequented the Melrose Diner, a South Philadelphia institution since the 1960s, cited by critics even today for its pies. His favorite was the lemon meringue, which served as a nice counterpoint to the hot dogs he'd just consumed while attending sports events nearby. Lemon meringue remains a popular selection throughout the diner world. It is the perfect marriage of sweet and tart. I love a robust lemon filling, and there is nothing half-hearted about this one. The other important feature here is the meringue topping. The egg whites are stabilized by the addition of a cornstarch paste, so that the meringue will hold up in the refrigerator—at home or at your favorite diner—without weeping, sagging, or throwing tantrums.

1. Make the pie crust pastry as directed and use half of it to line a 9-inch deep-dish pie plate. (Store the remaining disk for another use.) Fully bake the pie crust and let cool completely on a wire rack.

2. To make the lemon filling, in a medium nonreactive saucepan, stir together the sugar, cornstarch, and salt until well combined. Gradually whisk in the water until smooth. Place over medium-high heat and bring to a boil, whisking constantly. Remove the pan from the heat.

3. In a medium bowl, whisk the egg yolks until smooth. Whisk about $^1/_2$ cup of the hot cornstarch mixture into the yolks, then return the yolk mixture to the saucepan. Place over medium heat and bring to a gentle boil, whisking constantly. Continue to boil, whisking constantly, for 1 minute, or until very thick. Remove from the heat and

whisk in the lemon zest and juice and butter, whisking until the butter is completely melted. Whisk in the vanilla extract. Leave the filling in the saucepan off the heat while you prepare the meringue topping.

4. Position a rack in the upper third of the oven and preheat to 325°F. To make the meringue topping, in a small saucepan, combine the cornstarch and water. Place over medium heat and bring to a boil, stirring constantly. Allow the mixture to boil for 30 seconds, or until it is translucent. Whisk in the vanilla. Remove from the heat and set aside.

5. In the large bowl of an electric mixer, using the whisk attachment, beat the egg whites on medium-low speed until frothy. Add the salt and cream of tartar and increase the speed to medium-high. Beat the whites while gradually adding the sugar, 1 tablespoon at a time. Beat the whites on high speed until they are glossy but not dry. Whisk a scoop of the beaten whites into the cornstarch paste until blended. On low speed, beat the cornstarch mixture into the remaining whites, 1 tablespoon at a time. Increase the speed to medium-high and whip just until stiff peaks form.

6. To assemble the pie, place the pan containing the lemon filling over low heat to reheat for a minute. Scrape the hot filling into the baked pie crust and smooth the top.

7. Scrape the meringue into a large pastry bag fitted with a large star tip (such as Ateco #8). Pipe high dollops of the meringue on top of the pie, being careful to cover the filling completely by extending the meringue to the rim of the plate all around the edge. (Or you may pile the meringue on top of the pie and use the back of a tablespoon to create dramatic swirls.) Bake the pie for 15 to 18 minutes, or until golden brown. Let cool on a wire rack. Serve at room temperature or chilled.

Incredible Chocolate-Peanut Butter Pie

NUTTY WAFER CRUST

Vegetable oil for brushing pie plate

1³/₄ cups chocolate wafer crumbs

¹/₄ cup unsalted roasted peanuts, chopped

6 tablespoons (³/₄ stick) unsalted butter, melted

CHOCOLATE-PEANUT BUTTER FILLING

³/₄ cup granulated sugar

3 tablespoons cornstarch

2¹/₂ cups whole milk

3 large egg yolks

³/₄ cup crunchy peanut butter

2 ounces semisweet chocolate, chopped

1¹/₂ cups heavy cream

WHIPPED CREAM TOPPING

1 cup heavy cream

3 tablespoons granulated sugar

¹/₄ cup chopped unsalted roasted peanuts

This pie is creamy yet crunchy, with a light texture and intense flavor. It is for everyone who loves the celebrated combination of chocolate and peanut butter, a marriage made even more appealing by the addition of billowy whipped cream and chopped roasted peanuts. Make it when you're depressed, it's raining, and your favorite diner seems out of reach. It'll bring out the kid in you.

1. To make the nutty wafer crust, preheat the oven to 350°F. Lightly oil a 9-inch deep-dish pie plate. In a medium bowl, stir together the cookie crumbs, peanuts, and butter until well combined. Press the mixture evenly into the bottom and up the sides of the prepared pie plate. Bake the crust for 8 to 10 minutes, or until set. Cool on a wire rack.

2. To make the chocolate–peanut butter filling, in a medium saucepan, stir together the sugar and the cornstarch until well combined. Gradually whisk in the milk and egg yolks until smooth. Place over medium heat and bring to a gentle boil, whisking constantly. Continue to whisk for another minute, or until the mixture is thick. Remove from the heat and whisk in the peanut butter.

3. In a small bowl, combine 1 cup of the hot peanut butter mixture with the chopped chocolate and stir until the chocolate is melted. Scrape the mixture into the baked crust. Cover with plastic wrap, pressing it directly onto the surface, and chill for 1 hour, or until set. Transfer the remaining peanut butter mixture to a medium bowl, cover with plastic wrap, and chill for 45 minutes, or until cool but not set.

4. In a medium bowl, using a handheld electric mixer, beat the cream until soft peaks form. Using a rubber spatula, gently fold the cream into the cooled peanut butter mixture. Remove the plastic wrap. Scrape the mixture onto the chocolate filling and, using a small offset metal spatula, smooth into an even layer. Chill for 1 hour, or until set.

5. To make the whipped cream topping, in an electric mixer, using the whisk attachment or beaters, beat the cream on medium-low speed for 30 seconds. Increase the speed to medium-high and add the sugar. Beat until the cream forms soft peaks. Using a rubber spatula, pile the whipped cream evenly over the pie filling. Use the spatula to swirl the cream attractively over the pie. Sprinkle the peanuts over the cream. Chill the pie before serving.

Banana Brickle Cream Pie

CRUST
Basic Flaky Pie Crust (page 30)

BANANA FILLING
4 large egg yolks

$^1/_2$ cup granulated sugar

3 tablespoons cornstarch

$^1/_4$ teaspoon salt

$2^1/_2$ cups whole milk

2 tablespoons unsalted butter, cut into tablespoons

1 teaspoon vanilla extract

Pinch of ground cardamom (optional)

3 ripe, medium-sized bananas

1 teaspoon fresh lemon juice

GARNISH
$1^3/_4$ cups heavy cream

3 tablespoons confectioners' sugar, sifted

$^1/_2$ teaspoon vanilla extract

3 tablespoons English toffee bits such as Bits O'Brickle

Years ago, I spent my junior year in college in Bath, England. I vividly recall the time when my friend Steve Evans, a beefy Welsh rugby player, was celebrating a birthday, and I offered to bake him a cake. He looked at me sheepishly and inquired, "Do you know how to make banana cream pie? It's my favorite." I made two for him, and he ate them both. That day. Even the not-so-very-culinary Brits know a good thing when they taste it.

This pie is a slight variation of the Cadillac of cream pies. The addition of brickle adds a little crunch to an otherwise creamy and always scrumptious diner standard.

1. Make the pie crust pastry as directed and use half of it to line a 9-inch deep-dish pie plate. (Store the remaining disk for another use.) Fully bake the pie crust and let cool completely on a wire rack.

2. To make the banana filling, in a medium bowl, whisk together the egg yolks, granulated sugar, cornstarch, and salt until well combined; set aside. In a medium saucepan, bring the milk to a gentle boil over medium-low heat. Remove the pan from the heat and whisk about $^1/_2$ cup of the hot milk into the yolk mixture, then return the yolk mixture to the saucepan. Place over medium-high heat and bring to a gentle boil, whisking constantly. Continue to cook, whisking constantly, for 1 minute. Remove the pan from the heat and whisk in the butter pieces until melted. Whisk in the vanilla and the cardamom, if using. Quickly strain the custard through a fine-mesh sieve into a medium bowl. Half-fill a large bowl with ice cubes. Add cold water

to cover the cubes. Place the smaller bowl of custard in the ice "bath" and allow to cool, stirring occasionally, for several minutes.

3. Peel the bananas and slice them $^1/_4$ inch thick into a medium bowl. Add the lemon juice and toss gently to coat. Arrange the banana slices in an even layer in the bottom of the baked pie crust, pressing down on them lightly. Scrape the cooled custard filling over the bananas and smooth the top into an even layer with a spatula or the back of a spoon. Refrigerate the pie for at least 2 hours before topping and serving.

4. To garnish the pie, in an electric mixer, using the whisk attachment or beaters, beat the cream on medium-low speed for 30 seconds. Increase the speed to medium-high and add the sugar and vanilla. Beat until the cream forms soft peaks. Scrape the cream into a pastry bag fitted with a large star tip (such as Ateco #8). Pipe the cream over the custard in large rosettes, covering it completely. Sprinkle with the toffee bits. Serve the pie the day it is made.

Chocolate Chunk Pecan Pie

CRUST

Basic Flaky Pie Crust (page 30)

CHOCOLATE FILLING

4 large eggs

$^1/_2$ cup lightly packed light brown sugar

$^1/_2$ cup granulated sugar

1 cup light corn syrup

5 tablespoons unsalted butter, melted and cooled

2 teaspoons vanilla extract

$^1/_2$ teaspoon salt

1$^1/_2$ cups pecan halves, toasted (page 26)

3 ounces semisweet or bittersweet chocolate, cut into $^1/_8$-inch chunks

The fragrance of freshly baked pecan pie at a diner is both inviting and irresistible. But pecan pie can be cloyingly sweet. This recipe is less sweet than most and features the welcome addition of chocolate chunks, which melt into pockets of richness—a perfect foil to the crunchiness of the pecans. Serve this pie slightly warm with vanilla ice cream or whipped cream, if desired.

1. Make the pie crust pastry as directed and use half of it to line a 9-inch deep-dish pie plate. (Store the remaining disk for another use.) Refrigerate until needed.

2. Preheat the oven to 375°F. To make the chocolate filling, in a large bowl, whisk together the eggs, brown sugar, granulated sugar, corn syrup, melted butter, vanilla, and salt until well combined. Stir in the toasted nuts and chocolate chunks. Pour the filling into the prepared pie crust.

3. Bake the pie for 45 to 50 minutes, or until barely set; it should be slightly quivery. Cool on a wire rack for at least 1 hour, then refrigerate the pie until cold, about 2 hours. Slice the chilled pie and serve, or warm the slices in a 300°F oven before serving, if desired.

An old Southern favorite, sweet potato pie has become a staple on many diner menus across the country. This recipe produces a smooth, creamy pie with the delicious combination of sweet potato and warm spices. It is best served slightly warm, with lots of whipped cream dusted with cinnamon.

1. Make the pie crust pastry as directed and use half of it to line a 9-inch deep-dish pie plate. (Store the remaining disk for another use.) Partially bake the pie crust and cool completely on a wire rack.

2. Preheat the oven to 400°F. To make the sweet potato filling, in an electric mixer on medium-low speed, beat together the mashed sweet potatoes, sugar, spices, and salt until well combined. Add the whole eggs and the egg yolk, one at a time, beating well after each addition. Scrape down the sides of the bowl. Reduce the speed to low and add the milk, cream, lemon juice, melted butter, and vanilla. Beat until well combined.

3. Pour the filling into the baked pie shell. Bake the pie for 10 minutes; reduce the oven temperature to 325°F and bake for 50 minutes longer, or until set and a knife inserted near the edge of the pie comes out clean. Cool the pie on a wire rack. Serve the pie slightly warm.

CRUST

Basic Flaky Pie Crust (page 30)

SWEET POTATO FILLING

2 cups mashed cooked sweet potatoes (about $1^{1}/_{4}$ pounds sweet potatoes)

1 cup granulated sugar

$^{3}/_{4}$ teaspoon ground cinnamon

$^{1}/_{2}$ teaspoon ground ginger

$^{1}/_{4}$ teaspoon freshly grated nutmeg

$^{1}/_{8}$ teaspoon ground allspice

$^{1}/_{2}$ teaspoon salt

2 large whole eggs

1 large egg yolk

$^{3}/_{4}$ cup whole milk

$^{3}/_{4}$ cup heavy cream

1 teaspoon fresh lemon juice

3 tablespoons unsalted butter, melted and cooled

1 teaspoon vanilla extract

CHAPTER 5

Under the Cake Keeper

"All Baking Done on Premises." When I see that proclamation posted in a diner, I always order a piece of layer cake for dessert. The sign usually means that the cakes are fresh, moist, and flavorful. Displayed in a transparent cake keeper on the counter, the classic diner cake is tall, thickly frosted, and made from scratch. It is a variation on the same layer cakes that first appeared in this country in the latter half of the nineteenth century and continued to be popular until the late 1940s. Then came the invention of the cake mix, and made-from-scratch cakes became scarce. I became aware of the difference between "real" cakes and "cake-mix" cakes early in life.

When I was nine or ten, I made a "German" chocolate cake from a mix. It didn't come out as I had hoped. It was only about 2 inches high, with a thin, brownish icing, and not a pecan or shred of coconut in sight. I was heartbroken. But my mom, taking a positive approach, said it looked delicious and offered a piece to the plumber who had just fixed a leaky pipe under the sink. He readily accepted. I still remember the look of disappointment that crossed his face when he saw the cake. And when he took a bite, the look didn't go away. The cake wasn't what he had expected, either. And so I learned a lesson about cakes made from mixes. They never look as good as the picture on the box, and they don't even taste as good as they look.

The recipes in this chapter, for the most popular diner-style cakes, will not disappoint. They all look great and taste even better. None is difficult to make or requires unusual ingredients or equipment. Make one when you get a craving for something real, something that didn't come from a box. Or for a special occasion, like a birthday or anniversary. Or when you're expecting someone important, like the plumber.

Old-fashioned Jelly Roll

SPONGE CAKE

4 large eggs

$1/2$ teaspoon vanilla extract

$1/4$ cup plus 2 tablespoons granulated sugar

5 tablespoons unsalted butter, melted

1 cup sifted cake flour

$1/8$ teaspoon salt

1 teaspoon grated lemon zest

$1/4$ cup confectioners' sugar

FILLING

$3/4$ cup raspberry jam

1 tablespoon black raspberry liqueur such as Chambord

GARNISH

Confectioners' sugar for dusting

Whipped cream

Raspberries

My friend Belinda Brackenridge and her father had a cozy ritual when she was growing up. On the way to their summer house in Easthampton, New York, they would never fail to stop for a snack at the same diner. Belinda always had lemon meringue pie. Her father always had a slice of jelly roll. To celebrate this memory, Belinda once tried to make a jelly roll cake for her dad. It was a failure. The waxed paper she used to line the pan stuck to the sponge cake and Belinda ended up throwing it out. Here is a jelly roll Belinda can make successfully. It is simple, delicate, supremely light, and can be made in under an hour. Use the best-quality raspberry jam you can find, and serve the jelly roll with hot coffee. A scoop of vanilla ice cream is an excellent addition.

1. To make the sponge cake, preheat the oven to 375°F. Line the bottom of a $10^1/2$-by-$15^1/2$-by-1-inch jelly-roll pan with aluminum foil. Butter the foil and the sides of the pan.

2. In the bowl of an electric mixer, whisk together the eggs, vanilla, and sugar. Set the bowl over a saucepan of simmering water, making sure that the bottom of the bowl does not touch the water. Heat the egg mixture, whisking constantly, until the eggs are warm. Transfer the bowl to the electric mixer stand and, using the whisk attachment, beat on high speed for about 10 minutes, or until the mixture has tripled in volume. On low speed, beat in the melted butter in a thin stream.

3. In a medium bowl, stir together the flour, salt, and lemon zest. Remove the bowl containing the egg mixture from the mixer stand and, using a rubber spatula, fold in the dry

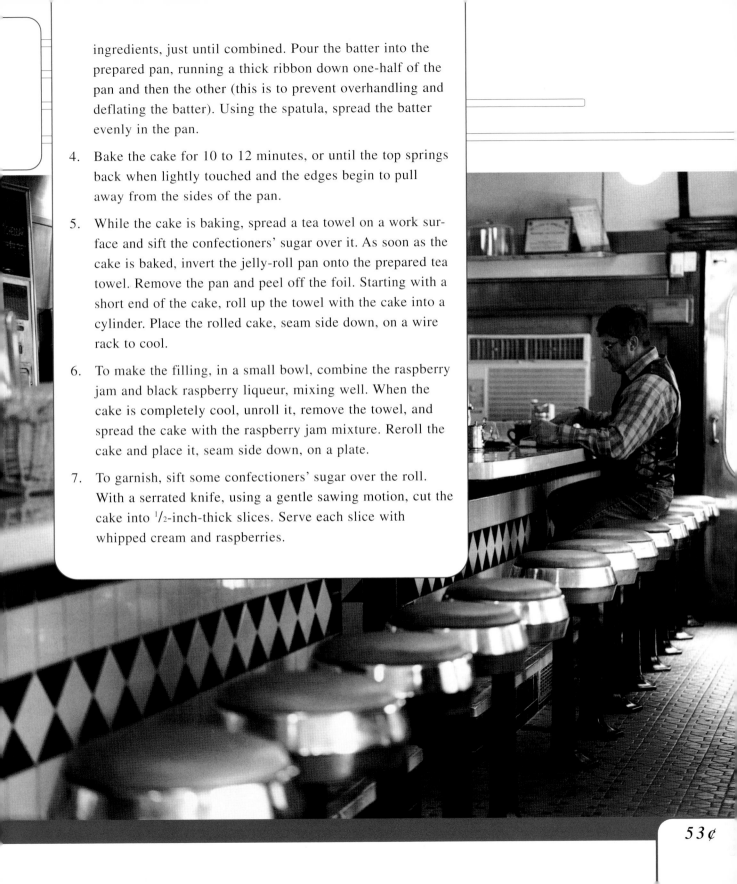

ingredients, just until combined. Pour the batter into the prepared pan, running a thick ribbon down one-half of the pan and then the other (this is to prevent overhandling and deflating the batter). Using the spatula, spread the batter evenly in the pan.

4. Bake the cake for 10 to 12 minutes, or until the top springs back when lightly touched and the edges begin to pull away from the sides of the pan.

5. While the cake is baking, spread a tea towel on a work surface and sift the confectioners' sugar over it. As soon as the cake is baked, invert the jelly-roll pan onto the prepared tea towel. Remove the pan and peel off the foil. Starting with a short end of the cake, roll up the towel with the cake into a cylinder. Place the rolled cake, seam side down, on a wire rack to cool.

6. To make the filling, in a small bowl, combine the raspberry jam and black raspberry liqueur, mixing well. When the cake is completely cool, unroll it, remove the towel, and spread the cake with the raspberry jam mixture. Reroll the cake and place it, seam side down, on a plate.

7. To garnish, sift some confectioners' sugar over the roll. With a serrated knife, using a gentle sawing motion, cut the cake into $1/2$-inch-thick slices. Serve each slice with whipped cream and raspberries.

53 ¢

High and Mighty White Cake

WHITE CAKE

2 cups cake flour

1 tablespoon baking powder

$^1/_2$ cup (1 stick) unsalted butter, slightly softened

$1^1/_2$ cups granulated sugar

1 teaspoon finely grated lemon zest

$1^1/_2$ teaspoons vanilla extract

1 teaspoon salt

9 large egg whites, at room temperature

1 cup whole milk

FROSTING

Fluffy White Frosting (page 74)

A diner in New York's Greenwich Village is bound to attract colorful characters, and the Tiffany Diner on West Fourth Street does not disappoint. It's busy during the day, but between three and five in the morning, when the nightclubs close, glittering swarms of drag queens, club kids, and other night phantoms take over the booths. After a night on the town, Martin Howard, a pastry chef, frequent club-goer, and Marilyn Monroe wanna-be, always saves room for an open face turkey sandwich with gravy and fries and a big piece of cake. Tiffany's cakes are as showy and decorated as the patrons and include flavors such as Black Forest, coconut, carrot, lemon, and Martin's personal favorite, a tall, thickly frosted vanilla white cake. Here is his version of that flashy three-layer tower.

1. To make the white cake, position 2 baking racks near the center of the oven and preheat to 350°F. Butter the bottom and sides of three 8-inch round cake pans. Cut out three 8-inch rounds of parchment or waxed paper and place a round in the bottom of each pan. Dust the sides of the pans with flour and tap out the excess.

2. In a medium bowl, sift together the cake flour and baking powder. Stir together the dry ingredients with a whisk. Set aside.

3. In an electric mixer, using the paddle attachment, beat the butter on medium-high speed until smooth, about 1 minute. On medium speed, gradually beat in $1^1/_4$ cups of the sugar. Increase the speed to high and beat until well combined, about 2 minutes. Add the lemon zest, vanilla, salt, and 3 of the egg whites. Scrape down the sides of the bowl with a

rubber spatula and beat the mixture on medium-high speed until light and fluffy, about 2 minutes. Add the sifted dry ingredients in 3 additions alternately with the milk in 3 additions. Scrape down the sides of the bowl and beat until smooth, about 1 minute.

4. In a clean bowl of the mixer, using the whisk attachment, beat the remaining 6 egg whites on medium-low speed until foamy. Increase the speed to medium-high and gradually beat in the remaining $\frac{1}{4}$ cup sugar. Continue to beat until the whites are stiff but not dry. Using a large rubber spatula, gently fold the beaten whites into the batter. Scrape the batter into the prepared pans.

5. Bake the cakes for 15 to 20 minutes, or until the tops spring back when lightly touched and a toothpick inserted into the center of each cake comes out clean. Cool the cakes in the pans on wire racks for 30 minutes. Invert the cakes onto the racks, peel off the paper, and cool completely.

6. Make the frosting. Place one cake layer on a serving plate. Scrape a generous amount of frosting over the cake, and, using a small offset metal spatula, spread it into an even layer. Top with another cake layer and repeat with another layer of frosting. Top with the remaining cake layer. Frost the top and sides of the cake with the remaining frosting. Serve the cake immediately, or refrigerate and bring to room temperature before serving.

German Chocolate Cake

CHOCOLATE CAKE

2$\frac{1}{4}$ cups cake flour

1 teaspoon baking soda

$\frac{1}{2}$ teaspoon salt

4 ounces sweet baking chocolate, chopped

$\frac{1}{2}$ cup coconut milk (not cream of coconut) or whole milk

1 cup buttermilk

2 teaspoons vanilla extract

1 cup (2 sticks) unsalted butter, slightly softened

1$\frac{3}{4}$ cups granulated sugar

4 large eggs, separated, at room temperature

$\frac{1}{4}$ teaspoon cream of tartar

COCONUT-PECAN FROSTING

1 cup heavy cream

1$\frac{1}{4}$ cups granulated sugar

4 large egg yolks, lightly beaten

$\frac{1}{2}$ cup (1 stick) unsalted butter, cut into tablespoons

1$\frac{1}{2}$ cups sweetened flaked dried coconut

1$\frac{1}{4}$ cups pecans, toasted (page 26) and chopped

There's nothing German about a German chocolate cake. The German refers to German's Sweet Chocolate, which was developed in this country by an Englishman named Sam German. Its popularity spread in the 1950s when a recipe was published in a Texas newspaper. This dark, sweet chocolate, a critical ingredient in the cake, is available in supermarkets under the Baker's label. In this recipe, light chocolate cake layers are stacked with a luscious coconut-pecan frosting spread between them.

1. To make the chocolate cake, position 2 baking racks near the center of the oven and preheat to 350°F. Butter the bottom and sides of three 8-inch round cake pans. Cut out three 8-inch rounds of parchment or waxed paper and place a round in the bottom of each pan. Dust the sides of the pans with flour and tap out the excess.

2. In a medium bowl, sift together the cake flour, baking soda, and salt. Stir together the dry ingredients with a whisk. Set aside.

3. In a small saucepan, heat the chocolate and coconut milk over medium-low heat, stirring constantly, until the chocolate is melted and the mixture is smooth. Remove the pan from the heat.

4. In a small bowl, stir together the buttermilk and vanilla.

5. In an electric mixer, using the paddle attachment, beat the butter on medium-high speed for about 1 minute, or until smooth. Gradually add 1$\frac{1}{2}$ cups of the sugar, 1 tablespoon at a time, and beat for about 3 minutes, or until very light. Beat in the egg yolks, one at a time, beating well after each

addition. Scrape down the sides of the bowl. Add the melted chocolate mixture and beat just until blended. Reduce the speed to low and add the flour mixture in 3 additions alternately with the buttermilk mixture in 2 additions. Beat until smooth. Scrape down the sides of the bowl as necessary.

6. In a clean bowl of the mixer, using the whisk attachment, beat the egg whites on medium-low speed until foamy. Add the cream of tartar and begin beating on medium-high speed. Gradually add the remaining $^1/_4$ cup sugar and beat until the meringue is stiff but not dry. Using a rubber spatula, gently fold the egg whites into the chocolate batter. Scrape the batter into the prepared pans.

7. Bake the cakes for 30 to 35 minutes, switching the pans from one rack to the other halfway through and baking them until a toothpick inserted into the center of each cake comes out clean. Cool the cakes in the pans on wire racks for 20 minutes. Invert the cakes onto the racks, peel off the paper, and cool completely.

8. Meanwhile, make the coconut-pecan frosting: In a medium saucepan, combine the cream, sugar, egg yolks, and butter. Cook over medium heat, stirring constantly, for about 6 minutes or until the mixture thickens and bubbles. Reduce the heat to low and cook for 2 minutes longer. Remove the pan from the heat and stir in the coconut and pecans. Cool for about 1 hour, or until the frosting is spreadable.

9. To assemble the cake, place 1 layer on a serving plate. Scrape about 1 scant cup of the frosting over the cake and, using a small offset metal spatula, spread it into an even layer. Top with another cake layer and repeat with another layer of frosting. Top with the remaining cake layer. Frost the top of the cake with the remaining frosting, letting it drip over the sides. Serve the cake immediately, or refrigerate and bring to room temperature before serving.

Toasted Almond Brittle Crunch Cake

WHITE CAKE

3$\frac{1}{2}$ cups sifted cake flour

4 teaspoons baking powder

$\frac{1}{2}$ teaspoon salt

1 cup (2 sticks) unsalted butter, slightly softened

2 cups granulated sugar

1 cup milk

$\frac{3}{4}$ teaspoon almond extract

8 large egg whites, at room temperature

ALMOND SOAKING SYRUP

$\frac{1}{4}$ cup granulated sugar

$\frac{1}{2}$ cup water

2 tablespoons amaretto liqueur, or
   1 teaspoon almond extract

1 teaspoon vanilla extract

ALMOND BRITTLE CRUNCH

1 cup granulated sugar

$\frac{1}{2}$ cup water

1 cup slivered blanched almonds, lightly toasted

INGREDIENTS CONTINUE >>

Inspired by Good Humor's toasted-almond ice cream bar, this cake is an updated diner dessert that will take you back to your childhood summer days. It does not skimp on the eggs, butter, or almond flavor. And like all respectable layer cakes, it is tall, slathered with frosting, and can easily stand up to the strongest cup of Joe.

1. To make the white cake, preheat the oven to 375°F. Butter the bottom and sides of two 9-inch round cake pans. Dust the pans with flour and tap out the excess.

2. In a large bowl, sift together the flour, baking powder, and salt. Stir together the dry ingredients with a whisk.

3. In the large bowl of an electric mixer, using the paddle attachment, beat the butter on medium-high speed for 2 minutes, or until creamy. Gradually add the sugar, 1 tablespoon at a time, and beat for about 3 minutes, or until very light.

4. Reduce the speed to low and add the dry ingredients to the batter in 3 additions alternately with the milk in 2 additions. Scrape down the sides of the bowl as necessary. Beat in the almond extract. Transfer the batter to a large mixing bowl.

5. In a clean, large bowl of the electric mixer, using the whisk attachment, beat the egg whites on medium-low speed until frothy. Increase the speed to medium-high and beat until stiff but not dry. Using a large rubber spatula, gently fold the beaten whites into the batter. Scrape the batter into the prepared pans and smooth the tops with the spatula.

6. Bake the cakes for 25 to 30 minutes, or until the tops spring back when lightly touched. Cool the cakes in the pans on wire racks for 10 minutes. Invert the cakes onto the racks and cool completely.

7. To make the almond soaking syrup, in a small saucepan, combine the sugar and water. Cook over medium heat, stirring constantly with a wooden spoon, until the sugar dissolves. Raise the heat to medium-high and bring the syrup to a boil. Remove the pan from the heat and cool the syrup. Stir in the amaretto or almond extract and vanilla.

8. To make the almond brittle crunch, lightly oil a large baking sheet. In a small saucepan, combine the sugar and water. Stir over medium heat until the sugar dissolves. Increase the heat to medium-high and continue to cook, without stirring, for 4 to 6 minutes, or until the syrup caramelizes. Immediately remove the pan from the heat. Quickly stir the slivered almonds into the hot caramel. Pour onto the baking sheet. Cool the brittle for 30 minutes, or until hard.

9. Coarsely chop the brittle on a cutting board using a large knife. Process the brittle in a food processor for 30 to 40 seconds, or until finely ground. Transfer to a small bowl.

10. To make the fluffy almond frosting, in a small, heavy saucepan, combine 1 cup of the sugar and the water and heat over medium-low heat, stirring constantly, until the sugar dissolves. Dip a clean pastry brush in warm water and wash down the sides of the pan to remove any sugar crystals. Raise the heat to medium-high and bring the mixture to a boil. Stop stirring and reduce the heat to low.

11. In a clean, large bowl of an electric mixer, using the whisk attachment, beat the egg whites on low speed until frothy. Add the cream of tartar, increase the speed to medium-high, and beat until soft peaks start to form. Gradually beat in the remaining 2 tablespoons sugar and beat until stiff peaks start to form.

RECIPE CONTINUES >>

FLUFFY ALMOND FROSTING

1 cup plus 2 tablespoons granulated sugar

$1/3$ cup water

5 large egg whites, at room temperature

$1/2$ teaspoon cream of tartar

1 pound (4 sticks) unsalted butter, softened

$1/2$ teaspoon almond extract

12. Increase the heat to high and cook the sugar syrup until it registers 240°F on a candy thermometer. While beating on medium-low speed, gradually pour the sugar syrup onto the beaten whites in a slow, steady stream near the side of the bowl. Increase the speed to medium-high and beat for 5 to 8 minutes, or until the mixture is completely cool and forms stiff, glossy peaks when the whisk is lifted.

13. One tablespoon at a time, beat in the softened butter on medium-high speed. (If the mixture looks curdled at any point, increase the speed to high and beat until smooth, then reduce the speed to medium-high and continue to beat in the butter.) Beat in the almond extract. (The frosting can be covered and stored at room temperature for up to 4 hours before assembling the cake.)

14. To assemble the cake, using a long, serrated knife, slice each cake layer in half horizontally to make 4 layers in all. Place 1 layer, cut side up, on a serving plate. Brush the layer with a generous amount of the almond soaking syrup. Using a small offset metal spatula, spread a thin layer of the almond frosting (about $1/2$ cup) onto the cake layer. Sprinkle evenly with $1/3$ cup of the brittle crunch. Top with another cake layer. Repeat the layering twice, soaking each cake layer and topping with frosting and brittle. Top with the final cake layer. Spread the remaining frosting evenly over the top and sides of the cake. Pat the remaining brittle crunch evenly around the sides and top of the cake, covering it almost completely. Serve the cake immediately, or refrigerate and bring to room temperature before serving.

Carrot Cake

Makes 10 servings

CARROT CAKE

2 cups all-purpose flour

1 tablespoon baking powder

1¼ teaspoons baking soda

¾ teaspoon salt

4 large eggs

1 cup granulated sugar

1¼ cups firmly packed light
  brown sugar

1½ cups vegetable oil

¼ cup heavy cream

1 tablespoon vanilla extract

1 tablespoon finely chopped
  crystallized ginger

1 tablespoon grated orange zest

1½ teaspoons ground cinnamon

¾ teaspoon freshly grated nutmeg

½ teaspoon ground cloves

3 cups firmly packed shredded carrots
  (about 4 medium carrots)

1 cup walnuts, chopped

INGREDIENTS CONTINUE >>

Carrot cake, which first became popular in this country in the 1960s, is now a national classic. It is as comfortable on a diner counter as it is on a menu in an elegant restaurant. My version is tall, moist, and full of nuts, ginger, and spice. It is frosted with a classic cream cheese frosting laced with fresh orange flavor.

1. To make the carrot cake, preheat the oven to 350°F. Butter the bottom and sides of three 8-inch round cake pans. Dust the pans with flour and tap out the excess.

2. In a medium bowl, sift together the flour, baking powder, baking soda, and salt. Stir together the dry ingredients with a whisk. Set aside.

3. In the bowl of an electric mixer on medium speed, beat together the eggs, granulated sugar, and light brown sugar until well combined. Add the oil, cream, vanilla, ginger, orange zest, and spices and continue to beat on low speed just until combined, scraping down the sides as necessary. Reduce the speed to low and beat in the flour mixture just until blended. Add the carrots and nuts and mix until blended. Scrape the batter into the prepared pans, and smooth the tops with a rubber spatula.

4. Bake the cakes for 40 to 45 minutes, or until dark golden brown and a toothpick inserted into the center of each cake comes out clean. Cool the cakes in the pans on wire racks for 20 minutes. Invert the cakes onto the racks and cool completely.

5. To make the cream cheese frosting, in an electric mixer on medium speed, beat together the cream cheese and butter until smooth. Reduce the speed to low and beat in the

CHAPTER 5: *UNDER THE CAKE KEEPER*

vanilla, orange juice and zest, and confectioners' sugar. Increase the speed to high and beat for about 30 seconds, or until smooth.

6. To assemble the cake, place 1 cake layer on a serving plate. Set aside $^3/_4$ cup of the frosting to garnish the top of the cake. Scrape about $^1/_2$ cup of the frosting over the cake layer and using a small offset metal spatula, spread it into an even layer. Top with another cake layer and repeat with another layer of frosting. Top with the remaining cake layer. Frost the top and sides of the cake with the remaining frosting. Scrape the reserved frosting into a pastry bag fitted with a large star tip (such as Ateco #8). Pipe 5 large rosettes on top of the cake. Sprinkle the top of the cake with the finely chopped walnuts. Serve the cake immediately, or refrigerate and bring to room temperature before serving.

CREAM CHEESE FROSTING

1 pound Philadelphia cream cheese, at room temperature

$^1/_2$ cup (1 stick) unsalted butter, at room temperature

1 teaspoon vanilla extract

2 teaspoons fresh orange juice

1 teaspoon grated orange zest

2 cups sifted confectioners' sugar

GARNISH

2 tablespoons finely chopped walnuts

FRA-RED BROILING   AIR CONDITIONED   VACULATOR COFF

63¢

Boston Cream Pie

CUSTARD FILLING

6 large egg yolks

$1/2$ cup granulated sugar

$1/3$ cup cornstarch, sifted

2 cups whole milk

3 tablespoons unsalted butter,
  cut into tablespoons

2 teaspoons vanilla extract

SPONGE CAKE

1 cup sifted cake flour

$1/2$ teaspoon salt

6 large eggs, at room temperature

$3/4$ cup granulated sugar

1 teaspoon grated lemon zest

$1^1/2$ teaspoons vanilla extract

6 tablespoons ($3/4$ stick) unsalted butter,
  melted and cooled

ASSEMBLY

$3/4$ cup heavy cream

CHOCOLATE GLAZE

4 ounces bittersweet chocolate, chopped

$1/2$ cup heavy cream

2 teaspoons instant espresso powder
  or instant coffee crystals

2 teaspoons hot water

1 teaspoon vanilla extract

New England is not only the birthplace of the diner, but also of Boston cream pie. Originating in the early nineteenth century, Boston pie, as it was then called, was a plain two-layer sponge cake filled with a vanilla custard. In 1855, a German-born pastry chef at Boston's Parker House Hotel spruced up the classic cake by adding a luscious chocolate glaze topping, and the dessert (now known as Boston cream pie) has remained popular to this day. In keeping with the diner tradition of tall cakes, my version consists of four layers filled with a deliciously light custard, leaving you to declare, "Who cares if they call it a pie when it's really a cake?"

1. To make the custard filling, in a medium bowl, whisk together the yolks, sugar, and cornstarch; set aside.

2. In a medium saucepan, bring the milk to a gentle boil. Remove the pan from the heat and whisk about $1/2$ cup of the hot milk into the yolk mixture. Return the entire mixture to the saucepan containing the remaining milk. Place over medium-high heat and bring to a boil, whisking constantly. Continue to boil, whisking constantly, for 1 minute, or until thick. Remove the pan from the heat, scrape the bottom of the pan with a spatula, and whisk until smooth. Whisk in the butter pieces until melted. Whisk in the vanilla. Quickly strain the custard through a fine-mesh sieve into a medium bowl. Cover with plastic wrap, pressing it directly onto the surface. Let cool to room temperature and then refrigerate for 2 hours, or until well chilled.

3. To make the sponge cake, preheat the oven to 350°F. Butter the bottom and sides of two 9-inch round cake pans. Dust the pans with flour and tap out the excess.

4. In a small bowl, stir together the flour and salt.

5. In the bowl of an electric mixer, whisk together the eggs and sugar. Set the bowl over a saucepan of simmering water, making sure that the bottom of the bowl does not touch the water. Heat the egg mixture, whisking constantly, until the eggs are warm. Transfer the bowl to the electric mixer stand and, using the whisk attachment, beat on high speed for about 10 minutes, or until the mixture has tripled in volume. Reduce the speed to low and beat in the lemon zest and vanilla.

6. Resift one-third of the flour mixture over the batter and gently fold it in with a rubber spatula. In two more additions, sift in the remaining flour mixture, again folding in gently. Place the melted butter in a small bowl. Scoop about $1/2$ cup of the cake batter into the bowl and stir until blended. Fold this mixture into the remaining cake batter. Scrape the batter into the prepared pans and smooth the tops with the spatula.

7. Bake the cakes for 28 to 30 minutes, or until the tops spring back when lightly touched. Cool the cakes in the pans on wire racks for 15 minutes. Invert the cakes onto the racks and cool completely.

8. To assemble the cake, using a long, serrated knife, cut each cake layer in half horizontally.

9. Remove the custard filling from the refrigerator and whisk until smooth.

10. In an electric mixer set on high speed, beat the heavy cream until it forms soft peaks. Fold one-third of the whipped cream into the custard to lighten it. Fold in the remaining cream.

RECIPE CONTINUES >>

11. Place 1 cake layer, cut side up, on a serving plate. Scrape about 1 cup of the custard filling onto the layer and, using a small offset metal spatula, spread it into an even layer. Repeat with the remaining cake layers and filling, ending with a cake layer. Refrigerate the cake while making the chocolate glaze.

12. To make the chocolate glaze, place the chocolate and the cream in a medium bowl and set the bowl over a saucepan of simmering water, making sure that the bottom of the bowl does not touch the water. Heat the mixture, stirring often, until the chocolate is melted and the mixture is smooth.

13. In a small container, dissolve the espresso powder or instant coffee in the hot water. Stir the coffee mixture and vanilla into the chocolate glaze.

14. Remove the cake from the refrigerator. Pour the warm glaze over the top of the cake, allowing some of it to drizzle down the sides. Serve the cake immediately, or refrigerate and bring to room temperature before serving.

67¢

Blue Ribbon Coconut Layer Cake

COCONUT CAKE

2¾ cups sifted cake flour

4 teaspoons baking powder

1 teaspoon salt

⅔ cup vegetable oil

¾ cup coconut milk

½ cup water

2 teaspoons coconut extract

1 teaspoon vanilla extract

4 large egg whites, at room temperature

¼ teaspoon cream of tartar

1½ cups granulated sugar

COCONUT FROSTING

1½ cups granulated sugar

2 large egg whites, at room temperature

¼ teaspoon cream of tartar

⅓ cup water

Pinch of salt

1 teaspoon coconut extract

ASSEMBLY

¾ cup seedless raspberry jam

2⅔ cups (one 7-ounce package) sweetened shredded dried coconut

Mabel's Diner in Piqua, Ohio, is the kind of good-natured place where you can ask for a doggie bag for anything—even the radish and parsley garnish from your burger platter. And Mary Schaaf Mulard, a Washington, D.C.–based food writer, is just the kind of woman who would ask. Mary frequented Mabel's during her college years. After late-night revelry, she and her friends noshed on triple-decker club sandwiches, burgers, crispy onion rings, and coconut cake. This is Mary's version of Mabel's extremely moist, knock-your-socks-off coconut cake. Coconut milk adds extra coconut flavor, while a thin coating of raspberry jam between the layers adds a colorful contrast.

1. To make the coconut cake, preheat the oven to 350°F. Butter the bottom and sides of two 8-inch round cake pans. Dust the pans with flour and tap out the excess.

2. In the bowl of an electric mixer, sift together the cake flour, baking powder, and salt.

3. In a medium bowl, whisk together the vegetable oil, coconut milk, water, coconut extract, and vanilla extract. Using the paddle attachment or beaters, begin blending the flour mixture on low speed. Gradually add the oil mixture, increase the speed to medium, and beat for 1 minute, or until the mixture is smooth, stopping once to scrape down the sides of the bowl.

4. In a clean bowl of the electric mixer, using the whisk attachment, beat the egg whites on medium-low speed until frothy. Add the cream of tartar and beat on medium-high speed until soft peaks form. Gradually add the sugar and

beat for 1 minute, or until the whites are shiny and firm (they will not form stiff peaks). Using a large rubber spatula, fold the beaten whites into the batter, one-third at a time. Scrape the batter into the prepared pans and spread it evenly with the spatula.

5. Bake the cakes for 25 to 30 minutes, or until a toothpick inserted into the center of each cake comes out clean. Cool the cakes in the pans on wire racks for 15 minutes. Invert the cakes onto the racks and cool completely.

6. To make the coconut frosting, in a large, deep bowl, combine the sugar, egg whites, cream of tartar, water, and salt. With a handheld electric mixer, beat the mixture until foamy, about 1 minute.

7. Place the bowl over a saucepan of simmering water, making sure that the water does not touch the bottom of the bowl. Beat constantly on low speed until the mixture reaches 160°F, about 7 minutes. Remove the bowl from the heat, add the coconut extract, and beat the frosting on high speed until it holds stiff peaks, about 7 minutes.

8. To assemble the cake, using a long, serrated knife, cut each layer in half horizontally. Place 1 layer, cut side up, on a serving plate. Using a small offset metal spatula, spread about one-third of the raspberry jam over the layer. Top with a large scoop of the frosting and spread it over the jam in an even layer. Repeat the layering, ending with the last cake layer. Frost the top and sides of the cake with the remaining coconut frosting. Sprinkle the coconut over the top and sides of the cake. Serve the cake immediately, or refrigerate and bring to room temperature before serving.

Chocolate Fudge Layer Cake

FUDGE CAKE

2 2/3 cups all-purpose flour

1 1/2 cups granulated sugar

1 cup firmly packed light brown sugar

1/2 cup unsweetened non-alkalized cocoa powder

2 teaspoons baking powder

1 teaspoon baking soda

1/2 teaspoon salt

3 large eggs, at room temperature

2/3 cup sour cream, at room temperature

1 tablespoon vanilla extract

3/4 cup (1 1/2 sticks) unsalted butter, melted and cooled

1/2 cup corn oil

1 1/4 cups ice water

FUDGE FROSTING

6 ounces unsweetened chocolate

1 cup (2 sticks) unsalted butter, softened

2 cups confectioners' sugar, sifted

1 tablespoon vanilla extract

This deep, dark cake is my version of the typical all-chocolate diner layer cake. Its intense chocolate flavor is balanced by the addition of sour cream and brown sugar, while corn oil and butter provide moistness. The rich, satiny fudge frosting completes the chocolate experience. Serve a slice with a glass of cold milk.

1. To make the fudge cake, preheat the oven to 350°F. Butter the bottom and sides of two 8-inch round cake pans. Dust the pans with flour and tap out the excess.

2. In a medium bowl, sift together the flour, sugars, cocoa, baking powder, baking soda, and salt. Stir the dry ingredients together with a whisk.

3. In a medium bowl, whisk together the eggs, sour cream, and vanilla until blended.

4. In the bowl of an electric mixer, using the paddle attachment or beaters, beat the melted butter and corn oil on low speed until blended. Beat in the water. Add the dry ingredients all at once and mix on low speed for about 1 minute, until blended. Scrape down the sides of the bowl with a rubber spatula. Add the egg mixture and mix for about 1 minute, or until blended. Scrape the batter into the prepared pans.

5. Bake the cakes for 50 to 55 minutes, or until a toothpick inserted into the center of each cake comes out clean. Cool the cakes in the pans on wire racks for 15 minutes. Invert the cakes onto the racks and cool completely.

6. To make the fudge frosting, put the chocolate in the top of a double boiler and melt over barely simmering water. Remove the top of the double boiler and let the chocolate cool.

7. In a bowl of the electric mixer, using the paddle attachment, beat the butter on medium-high speed for about 1 minute, or until creamy. Add the sifted confectioners' sugar and beat for about 2 minutes, or until well blended and light. Beat in the vanilla extract. Reduce the speed to low and beat in the cooled chocolate. Increase the speed to medium-high and beat for about 1 minute, or until glossy and smooth.

8. To assemble the cake, using a long, serrated knife, slice off the domed top of each cake layer, so that the cakes are flat. Place the cake scraps in a food processor and process for 20 seconds, until the scraps are fine crumbs. Set the crumbs aside.

9. Place 1 cake layer on a serving plate. Scrape about $^1/_2$ cup of the frosting over the cake and, using a small offset metal spatula, spread it into an even layer. Top with the second cake layer. Frost the top and sides of the cake with the remaining frosting. Sprinkle the top of the cake with some of the reserved cake crumbs. Pat the remaining cake crumbs around the sides of the cake. Serve the cake immediately, or refrigerate and bring to room temperature before serving.

Lemon Layer Cake

LEMON CAKE

2¹/₂ cups cake flour

2 teaspoons baking powder

¹/₂ teaspoon baking soda

¹/₄ teaspoon salt

1 cup (2 sticks) unsalted butter, slightly softened

1¹/₂ cups granulated sugar

2 large whole eggs, at room temperature

3 large egg yolks, at room temperature

2 teaspoons vanilla extract

1 teaspoon grated lemon zest

¹/₄ cup fresh lemon juice

¹/₂ cup whole milk

LEMON FILLING

2 large egg yolks

¹/₃ cup granulated sugar

¹/₄ cup fresh lemon juice

2 tablespoons unsalted butter, slightly softened

Pinch of salt

1 teaspoon finely grated lemon zest

¹/₂ cup heavy cream

INGREDIENTS CONTINUE >>

Although its style varies from diner to diner, lemon layer cake is a regular item on the lunch counter. This version is full of pure lemon flavor: moist lemon cake layers filled with a tart, creamy filling, all covered with a lemon buttercream frosting. Serve with good-quality vanilla ice cream, if you like.

1. To make the lemon cake, preheat the oven to 350°F. Butter the bottom and sides of two 9-inch round cake pans. Dust the pans with flour and tap out the excess.

2. In a medium bowl, sift together the flour, baking powder, baking soda, and salt. Stir together the dry ingredients with a whisk. Set aside.

3. In an electric stand mixer, using the paddle attachment or beaters, beat the butter on medium speed for about 30 seconds, or until creamy. Gradually add the sugar, increase the speed to medium-high, and continue to beat until the mixture is light, about 3 minutes. Scrape down the sides of the bowl.

4. Add the whole eggs and egg yolks, one at a time, beating well after each addition. Beat in the vanilla and lemon zest. Reduce the speed to low and gradually beat in the lemon juice (the batter will appear curdled at this point but will smooth out after you add the dry ingredients). Beat in the dry ingredients in 3 additions alternately with the milk in 2 additions. Scrape down the sides of the bowl and beat for another 10 seconds. Scrape the batter into the prepared pans.

5. Bake the cakes for 20 to 25 minutes, or until a toothpick inserted into the center of each cake comes out clean.

Cool the cakes in the pans on wire racks for 20 minutes. Invert the cakes onto the racks and cool completely.

6.   To make the lemon filling, in a medium nonreactive saucepan, whisk together the yolks and sugar until combined. Whisk in the lemon juice, butter, and salt. Cook over medium-low heat, stirring constantly with a wooden spoon, for 5 to 6 minutes, or until the mixture turns opaque, thickens, and coats the back of the spoon. Do not let the filling boil, or it will curdle. Pour the mixture through a fine-mesh sieve into a medium bowl. Stir in the lemon zest and allow the filling to cool.

7.   Cover with plastic wrap, pressing directly onto the surface, and refrigerate for 1 hour, or until chilled.

8.   In a clean bowl of the electric mixer, using the whisk attachment or beaters, beat the heavy cream on high speed until soft peaks form. Remove the lemon filling from the refrigerator and whisk until smooth. Using a rubber spatula, gently fold the whipped cream into the filling. Cover the bowl and refrigerate the filling until ready to assemble the cake.

9.   To make the lemon frosting, in the large bowl of the electric mixer, using the paddle attachment or beaters, beat the butter on medium speed until creamy, about 30 seconds. Gradually beat in the confectioners' sugar on low speed. Add the cream, lemon juice, vanilla, and lemon zest. Increase the speed to medium-high, and beat for about 3 minutes, or until the frosting is light and fluffy.

10.   To assemble the cake, place 1 cake layer on a serving plate. Pile the lemon filling onto the center using a small offset metal spatula, and spread it into an even layer, leaving a 1-inch border around the edge of the cake layer. Top with the second cake layer. Frost the top and sides of the cake with the lemon frosting. (If some of the filling oozes out from the middle, just blend it with the frosting around the sides of the cake.) Serve the cake immediately, or refrigerate and bring to room temperature before serving.

LEMON FROSTING

$^3/_4$ cup (1$^1/_2$ sticks) unsalted butter, softened

3$^1/_2$ cups confectioners' sugar

2 tablespoons heavy cream

2 teaspoons fresh lemon juice

$^1/_4$ teaspoon vanilla extract

1 teaspoon finely grated lemon zest

Devil's Food Cake with Fluffy White Frosting

DEVIL'S FOOD CAKE

2^1/$_4$ cups granulated sugar

1^3/$_4$ cups cake flour

1^1/$_4$ cups unsweetened non-alkalized
   cocoa powder

2^1/$_4$ teaspoons baking soda

1^1/$_4$ teaspoons baking powder

^{1}/$_2$ teaspoon salt

3 large whole eggs

1 large egg yolk

1 tablespoon vanilla extract

^{1}/$_2$ cup (1 stick) plus 1 tablespoon
   unsalted butter, melted and cooled

1^1/$_2$ cups buttermilk

^{3}/$_4$ cup strongly brewed coffee, cooled

RICH CHOCOLATE FILLING

9 ounces semisweet chocolate, chopped

1 cup heavy cream

1 teaspoon vanilla extract

FLUFFY WHITE FROSTING

5 large egg whites

1^3/$_4$ cups granulated sugar

^{1}/$_3$ cup water

^{1}/$_2$ teaspoon cream of tartar

2 teaspoons vanilla extract

It'll be a cold day in Hell before you'll find a diner menu without devil's food cake on it. This American classic gets its name from its slightly reddish brown color, caused by the reaction of alkaline baking soda with acidic chocolate. In this recipe, intense chocolate flavor is balanced by the addition of buttermilk and coffee, while butter provides moistness. A rich, satiny chocolate filling and clouds of billowy white frosting completes the sinful experience. Ice-cold milk is the mandatory accompaniment.

1. To make the devil's food cake, preheat the oven to 350°F. Butter the bottom and sides of two 9-inch round cake pans. Dust the pans with flour and tap out the excess.

2. In a large mixing bowl, sift together the sugar, cake flour, cocoa powder, baking soda, baking powder, and salt. Stir together the dry ingredients with a whisk and set aside.

3. In a medium mixing bowl, whisk together the whole eggs and the egg yolk until combined. Whisk in the vanilla and the melted butter. Whisk in the buttermilk and coffee. Pour the buttermilk into the dry ingredients and whisk just until smooth. Scrape the batter into the prepared pans.

4. Bake the cakes for 30 to 35 minutes, or until the edges of the cakes pull away from the sides of the pans and a toothpick inserted into the center of each cake comes out clean. Cool the cakes in the pans on wire racks for 20 minutes. Invert the cakes onto racks and cool completely.

5. To make the rich chocolate filling, place the chocolate in a medium bowl. In a medium saucepan, heat the cream until it comes to a gentle boil. Pour the hot cream over the chopped

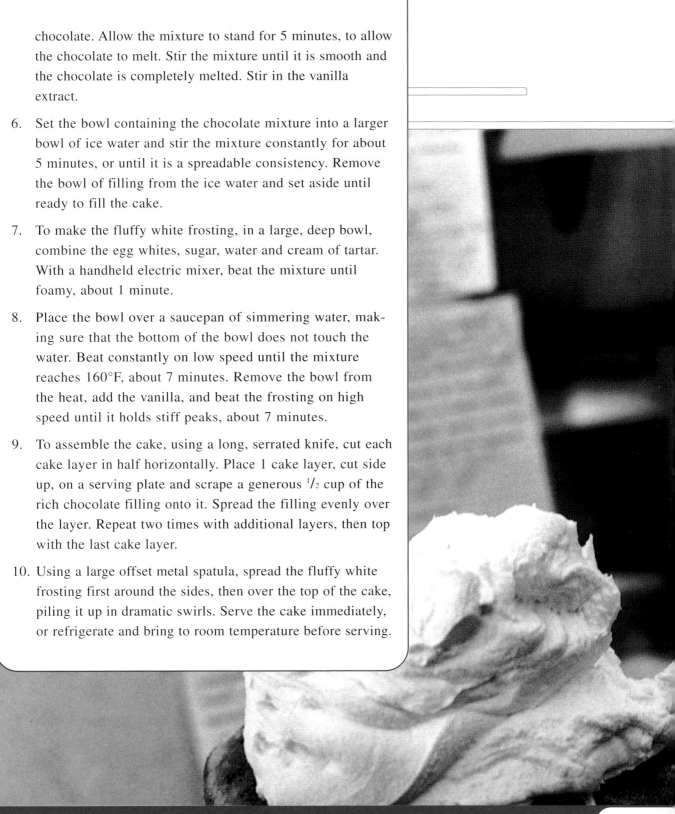

chocolate. Allow the mixture to stand for 5 minutes, to allow the chocolate to melt. Stir the mixture until it is smooth and the chocolate is completely melted. Stir in the vanilla extract.

6. Set the bowl containing the chocolate mixture into a larger bowl of ice water and stir the mixture constantly for about 5 minutes, or until it is a spreadable consistency. Remove the bowl of filling from the ice water and set aside until ready to fill the cake.

7. To make the fluffy white frosting, in a large, deep bowl, combine the egg whites, sugar, water and cream of tartar. With a handheld electric mixer, beat the mixture until foamy, about 1 minute.

8. Place the bowl over a saucepan of simmering water, making sure that the bottom of the bowl does not touch the water. Beat constantly on low speed until the mixture reaches 160°F, about 7 minutes. Remove the bowl from the heat, add the vanilla, and beat the frosting on high speed until it holds stiff peaks, about 7 minutes.

9. To assemble the cake, using a long, serrated knife, cut each cake layer in half horizontally. Place 1 cake layer, cut side up, on a serving plate and scrape a generous $^1/_2$ cup of the rich chocolate filling onto it. Spread the filling evenly over the layer. Repeat two times with additional layers, then top with the last cake layer.

10. Using a large offset metal spatula, spread the fluffy white frosting first around the sides, then over the top of the cake, piling it up in dramatic swirls. Serve the cake immediately, or refrigerate and bring to room temperature before serving.

Maple-Walnut Cake

MAPLE CAKE

$1^1/_2$ cups walnuts, toasted (page 26)

$2^1/_4$ cups sifted cake flour

$2^1/_2$ teaspoons baking powder

1 teaspoon ground cinnamon

$^1/_2$ teaspoon salt

$1^1/_4$ cups ($2^1/_2$ sticks) unsalted butter, slightly softened

$1^1/_2$ cups granulated sugar

4 large eggs

1 tablespoon vanilla extract

$^3/_4$ teaspoon maple flavoring

$^1/_2$ cup strongly brewed coffee, cooled

MAPLE COFFEE FROSTING

5 large egg whites

2 cups granulated sugar

$^1/_2$ cup water

2 cups (4 sticks) unsalted butter, softened

2 teaspoons instant espresso powder dissolved in 1 tablespoon hot water and cooled

$^1/_4$ teaspoon maple flavoring

2 teaspoons vanilla extract

Maple is a true New England flavor, and every diner menu in the region features at least one maple-flavored dessert. This cake combines maple with toasted walnuts and coffee, in luscious, buttery layers. It is best served at room temperature with, naturally, hot coffee.

1. To make the maple cake, preheat the oven to 350°F. Butter and flour two 9-inch round cake pans.

2. Place the walnuts and $^1/_4$ cup of the cake flour in a food processor. Process until the nuts are finely ground, about 45 seconds. Transfer the nut mixture to a medium bowl. Sift the remaining cake flour, baking powder, cinnamon, and salt over the nut mixture. Using a large spoon, stir the dry ingredients until well combined.

3. In the bowl of an electric mixer, using the paddle attachment, beat the butter on high speed until creamy, about 30 seconds. Add the sugar, 1 tablespoon at a time, and beat on high speed until light, about 5 minutes. Beat in the eggs, one at a time, waiting until each egg is incorporated before adding the next. Using a rubber spatula, scrape down the sides of the bowl. Beat the mixture for another 30 seconds.

4. Stir the vanilla extract and maple flavoring into the cooled coffee. While mixing on low speed, add the sifted dry ingredients in 3 additions alternately with the coffee mixture in 2 additions. Scrape the batter into the prepared pans.

5. Bake the cakes for 30 to 35 minutes, or until a toothpick inserted in the center of each cake comes out clean. Cool the cakes on wire racks for 30 minutes. Invert the cakes onto the racks and cool completely while making the frosting.

6. To make the maple-coffee frosting, place the egg whites in the bowl of an electric mixer. Set the bowl over a larger bowl or pot of hot water. Swirl the bowl of whites several times so that the whites absorb the warmth of the water. Leave the bowl in the water and set aside.

7. In a medium, heavy-bottomed saucepan, combine the sugar and the water. Cook over medium-high heat, stirring constantly, until the sugar is completely dissolved. Bring the mixture to a boil and cook, without stirring, until the syrup reaches 234°F on a candy thermometer. Reduce the heat to low and begin beating the egg whites.

8. Place the bowl of egg whites in the mixer stand and beat on medium speed until frothy. Increase the speed to high and beat until the whites form soft peaks. Turn the mixer off. Increase the heat under the sugar syrup to high and cook until it reaches 240°F (soft ball stage). Immediately remove it from the heat and, with the mixer running on medium speed, carefully pour the hot syrup down the side of the bowl into the beating egg whites. Continue to beat the whites for 7 to 8 minutes or until they are cool.

9. With the mixer running on medium speed, beat in the butter, 1 tablespoon at a time. The mixture will appear lumpy when half the butter has been added, but it will smooth out when it has all been added. Stir the extracts into the dissolved coffee and beat this into the frosting. (The frosting may be made up to 2 days in advance and stored in the refrigerator; allow it to come to room temperature before using.)

RECIPE CONTINUES >>

10. To assemble the cake, using a long, serrated knife, cut each cake layer in half horizontally. Place 1 cake layer, cut side up, on a serving plate. Set aside $^1/_2$ cup of the frosting to garnish the top of the cake. Scrape a generous $^1/_2$ cup of the frosting over the cake layer and, using a small offset metal spatula, spread it into an even layer. Top with a second layer and repeat the layering twice, ending with the last cake layer. Frost the top and sides of the cake with the remaining frosting.

11. Using a large offset metal spatula that has been dipped in hot water and wiped dry, smooth the sides of the cake as much as possible so that no ridges remain in the frosting. Drag a cake comb or serrated knife around the sides of the cake in an up-and-down motion to create decorative wavy lines. Spoon the reserved $^1/_2$ cup frosting in a pastry bag fitted with a large star tip (such as Ateco #8) and pipe 8 rosettes around the top edge of the cake. Serve the cake immediately, or refrigerate and bring to room temperature before serving.

79¢

CHAPTER 6

Say Cheesecake

Cream cheese, puttylike and pedestrian, is an unlikely candidate for culinary stardom. But as the primary ingredient in cheesecake, this distinctively tangy and dense-textured cheese has a lofty stature among diner dessert aficionados.

Cheesecake first became popular in this country in the late nineteenth century, after a couple of dairy farmers from upstate New York developed a rich, cream-based cheese, inspired by the French neufchâtel. Recipes for a cake that showcased its richness soon appeared, and an American dessert classic was born. Cheesecake has always fit in with the diner philosophy of simple excess. Unadorned, cheesecake is sumptuous. Topped with a basic fruit or chocolate glaze, it is more so. At one time or another, you've probably stood mesmerized, gazing into the glass dessert case at the front of a diner, admiring the stunning variety of cheesecakes. While purists may bristle at the notion of anything but plain cheesecake, the more adventurous appreciate assorted add-ins, flavor enhancements, and fruit toppings. Diners can satisfy all tastes.

While I have varied the techniques for making the cakes featured in this chapter, most are baked for a short time at a relatively high temperature and then at a low temperature for a long period. Some are baked in a water bath, while others don't require it. The common denominator among the techniques is that the process should never be rushed. A perfect cheesecake takes a couple of hours to produce and should chill for at least 4 hours, or preferably overnight, before being served. Cheesecake can be made up to a day in advance and in fact improves in flavor and texture when allowed to stand in the refrigerator for a day. For consistent results, use Philadelphia brand cream cheese.

Classic Diner Cheesecake

GRAHAM CRACKER CRUST

1¼ cups graham cracker crumbs

¼ cup granulated sugar

¼ cup (½ stick) unsalted butter, softened

CHEESECAKE FILLING

1½ cups granulated sugar

3 tablespoons all-purpose flour

2 pounds cream cheese, at room temperature

1 tablespoon vanilla extract

5 large eggs

½ cup sour cream

½ cup heavy cream

1 teaspoon lemon zest

A famous French chef once told me about his first visit to an American diner. His English was still a little shaky then, and when the waitress suggested cheesecake for dessert, he nodded enthusiastically. Moments later, he was presented with a pale, dense slab of he knew not what, instead of what he expected: a selection of cheeses. Adventurous by nature, he ate his first piece of American-style cheesecake and has been a devotee ever since.

Also known as New York cheesecake, this cake is the gold standard of diner cheesecakes. It's rich and smooth, with a subtle sour cream tang. Unlike most cheesecakes, you bake it in a very hot oven for a short period, then lower the temperature and bake it for an additional hour. The cake cools in the oven for another hour, and then must be chilled for at least 4 hours. Making it is a big investment in time, but the results are well worth it. Bake it a day ahead if you like; the flavor will only improve. Beats the cheese platter every time.

1. To make the graham cracker crust, preheat the oven to 500°F. Place an oven thermometer in the oven.

2. In a medium bowl, combine the graham cracker crumbs and sugar. Add the butter and, using a fork, work it into the graham cracker mixture until completely combined. Scrape the crumb mixture into a 9-inch springform pan and pat it evenly over the bottom of the pan.

3. To make the cheesecake filling, in a medium bowl, stir together the sugar and flour; set aside.

4. In an electric mixer, using the paddle attachment or beaters, beat the cream cheese on low speed until smooth. Beat in the vanilla. Add the sugar mixture, 1 heaping tablespoon at a time, beating on low speed. Scrape down the sides of the bowl. Add the eggs, one at a time, beating well after each addition and stopping to scrape down the sides of the bowl as necessary. Beat in the sour cream, heavy cream, and lemon zest. Scrape the batter into the prepared pan.

5. Bake the cake for 10 minutes. Reduce the heat to 200°F and open the oven door until the oven thermometer registers 200°F. Close the door and continue to bake at this temperature for 1 hour. Turn the oven off and, with a wooden spoon, prop the door open slightly. Leave the cheesecake in the warm oven for an additional hour. Transfer the cheesecake to a wire rack and cool completely. Refrigerate the cake, covered with plastic wrap, for at least 4 hours before serving.

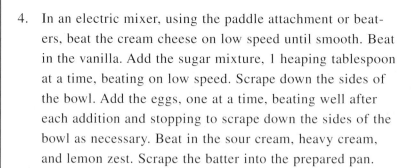

Strawberry Shortcrust Cheesecake

Makes 12 to 16 servings

SHORTCRUST

1³/₄ cups cake flour

¹/₂ cup confectioners' sugar

¹/₈ teaspoon salt

¹/₂ cup (1 stick) plus 3 tablespoons
unsalted butter, softened, cut into
tablespoons

CHEESECAKE FILLING

1¹/₂ pounds cream cheese, softened

1¹/₄ cups granulated sugar

1 tablespoon cornstarch, sifted

3 large eggs

2 teaspoons vanilla extract

1 teaspoon grated lemon zest

¹/₄ teaspoon salt

2 cups sour cream

STRAWBERRY TOPPING

2 pints strawberries, hulled

¹/₂ cup granulated sugar

2 tablespoons water

2 teaspoons cornstarch

1 teaspoon fresh lemon juice

1 tablespoon unsalted butter

With the exception of the Classic Diner Cheesecake (page 82), this is the most popular lunch-counter cheesecake. Dense and rich, topped with gleaming whole strawberries, this gem stands out in any diner's refrigerated glass case. The buttery shortcrust the cake rests on complements the tang of the berries nicely.

1. To make the shortcrust, preheat the oven to 350°F. Butter the bottom and sides of a 9-inch springform pan.

2. In an electric mixer, using the paddle attachment, beat together the cake flour, confectioners' sugar, and salt on low speed until blended. Scatter the butter over the dry ingredients and beat on low speed until the dough starts to come together, about 1 minute. Turn the dough out onto a lightly floured surface and shape it into a thick disk. Lightly dust the disk with flour. Roll out into a 9-inch round and place it in the bottom of the prepared pan. With your fingers, smooth out any uneven spots in the crust. Using a fork, lightly press down around the edges. Prick the crust well all over with a fork.

3. Bake the crust for 20 to 25 minutes, or until lightly browned around the edges. Cool the crust on a wire rack. Leave the oven on.

4. To make the cheesecake filling, in the electric mixer, using the paddle attachment, beat the cream cheese and sugar on medium-low speed until smooth and creamy, about 2 minutes. Beat in the cornstarch. Add the eggs, one at a time, beating well after each addition and stopping to scrape down the sides of the bowl as necessary. Beat in the vanilla, lemon zest, and salt until blended. Add the sour cream and mix just until blended.

5. Using heavy-duty aluminum foil, double-wrap the outside of the springform pan containing the cooled shortcrust (this will prevent water from seeping into the crust when it is baked). Scrape the filling into the prepared pan, smooth the top with a rubber spatula, and place the pan in a large roasting pan. Pour hot water to a depth of about 1 inch into the roasting pan. Bake the cake for 50 minutes. Turn the oven off (without opening the door) and leave the cake in the closed oven for an additional hour. Remove the cake from the water bath, peel off the foil, place the pan on a wire rack, and cool completely. Chill the cheesecake, covered with plastic wrap, for at least 4 hours or up to 24 hours.

6. To make the strawberry topping, select the best-looking strawberries and place them (make sure they are dry), pointed side up, on top of the chilled cheesecake, covering it completely. Place the remaining berries (there should be about $^1/_2$ pint) in a medium saucepan. Add the sugar and 1 tablespoon of the water and cook the mixture over medium heat, stirring constantly, for about 5 minutes, or until the berries are softened and have given off their juice. Strain the berries through a sieve into a bowl, pressing down on them to remove as much juice as possible. Return the juice to the saucepan and discard the berries. In a small bowl, stir together the cornstarch and the remaining 1 tablespoon water. Add the cornstarch mixture to the strawberry juice and cook over medium heat, stirring constantly, until it comes to a boil. Allow the mixture to boil for 1 minute, stirring constantly. Remove the pan from the heat and stir in the lemon juice and butter. Allow the strawberry mixture to cool for about 10 minutes, or until just warm.

7. Brush the warm topping generously over the strawberries, allowing it to spill over onto the top of the cake. Return the cake to the refrigerator for about 30 minutes, or until the topping is set, before serving.

Cherry Cheesecake

CAKE BASE

Sponge cake from Old-fashioned Jelly Roll (page 52), prepared through step 4 and cooled

CHEESECAKE FILLING

2 pounds cream cheese, softened

1$^1/_4$ cups granulated sugar

4 large eggs

1 tablespoon cornstarch, sifted

3 tablespoons freshly squeezed lemon juice

2 teaspoons vanilla extract

$^1/_4$ teaspoon salt

2$^1/_2$ cups sour cream

CHERRY TOPPING

1 can (16 ounces) pitted sour red cherries in water

2 tablespoons granulated sugar

1 tablespoon cornstarch

$^1/_4$ cup water

1 tablespoon unsalted butter

$^1/_4$ teaspoon almond extract

A few drops of red food coloring

A tart cherry topping is the perfect foil for a sweet, rich cheesecake, and no respectable diner would be without this combination on its menu. Make sure to use sour cherries rather than the sweet, dark variety. The sponge cake base is a welcome change from a crumb crust and soaks up some of the cherry flavor.

1. Make the sponge cake as directed. After baking, remove from the oven, invert onto a wire rack, remove the pan, peel off the foil, and let cool completely.

2. Preheat the oven to 350°F. Butter the bottom and sides of a 9-inch springform pan. Using the bottom of the springform pan as a guide and a small, sharp knife, cut out a 9-inch round from the sponge cake. Place about one-third of the cake scraps in a food processor and process until finely ground. Dust the sides (not the bottom) of the pan with the crumbs. Place the cake round in the bottom of the springform pan.

3. To make the cheesecake filling, in an electric mixer, using the paddle attachment or beaters, beat the cream cheese and sugar on medium-low speed until smooth and creamy, about 2 minutes. Add the eggs, one at a time, beating well after each addition and stopping to scrape down the sides of the bowl as necessary. Beat in the cornstarch, lemon juice, vanilla, and salt until blended. Beat in the sour cream on low speed just until blended. Pour the batter into the prepared pan (it will fill the pan).

4. Bake the cake for 20 minutes. Reduce the oven temperature to 225°F and bake for an additional 1$^1/_2$ hours, or just until the center no longer looks wet. Turn the oven off (without

opening the door), and leave the cake in the closed oven for an additional hour. Remove the cake from the oven and cool on a wire rack for 30 minutes. Chill the cheesecake, covered with plastic wrap, for at least 3 hours or up to 24 hours.

5. To make the cherry topping, drain the cherries, reserving $1/2$ cup of the liquid. In a small saucepan, combine the sugar and cornstarch. Slowly whisk in the cherry liquid and the water. Bring the mixture to a boil over medium heat, stirring constantly. Continue to boil, stirring, for 1 minute. Remove the pan from the heat and stir in the butter and almond extract. Stir in the cherries and just enough red food coloring to brighten the topping. Cool the mixture to room temperature.

6. Pour the cooled topping over the cheesecake, making sure that it is completely covered. Chill the cake for at least 2 hours before serving.

Blueberry-Lemon Cheesecake with a Gingersnap Crust

GINGERSNAP CRUST

1³/₄ cups gingersnap crumbs

1 tablespoon granulated sugar

5 tablespoons unsalted butter, melted

LEMON CHEESECAKE FILLING

1¹/₂ pounds cream cheese, softened

1¹/₄ cups granulated sugar

1 tablespoon cornstarch, sifted

3 large eggs

2 teaspoons grated lemon zest

2 tablespoons fresh lemon juice

2 cups sour cream

BLUEBERRY TOPPING

3 cups blueberries

¹/₂ cup granulated sugar

2 teaspoons cornstarch

1 tablespoon water

1 teaspoon fresh lemon juice

A blueberry topping heightens the tartness of this lemon cheese-cake. The crust, made from gingersnap cookies, adds a spicy dimension and complements the lemon flavor. Make this cake when blueberries are in season, June through August.

1. To make the gingersnap crust, preheat the oven to 350°F. Butter the bottom and sides of a 9-inch springform pan. Cut out a 9-inch round of parchment or waxed paper and place it in the bottom of the pan. Butter the paper. Using heavy-duty aluminum foil, double-wrap the outside of the pan.

2. In a medium bowl, combine the gingersnap crumbs and sugar. Stir in the melted butter until evenly combined. Pat the crumb mixture onto the bottom of the prepared pan in an even layer. Refrigerate the crust while you make the filling.

3. To make the lemon cheesecake filling, in an electric mixer, using the paddle attachment, beat the cream cheese and sugar on medium-low speed until smooth and creamy, about 2 minutes. Beat in the cornstarch until blended. Add the eggs, one at a time, beating well after each addition and stopping to scrape down the sides of the bowl as necessary. Beat in the lemon zest and lemon juice. Add the sour cream and mix just until blended. Scrape the filling into the pre-pared pan, smooth the top with a rubber spatula, and place the pan in a large roasting pan. Pour hot water to a depth of about 1 inch into the roasting pan.

4. Bake the cake for 50 minutes. Turn the oven off (without opening the door) and leave the cake in the closed oven for an additional hour. Remove the cake from the water bath,

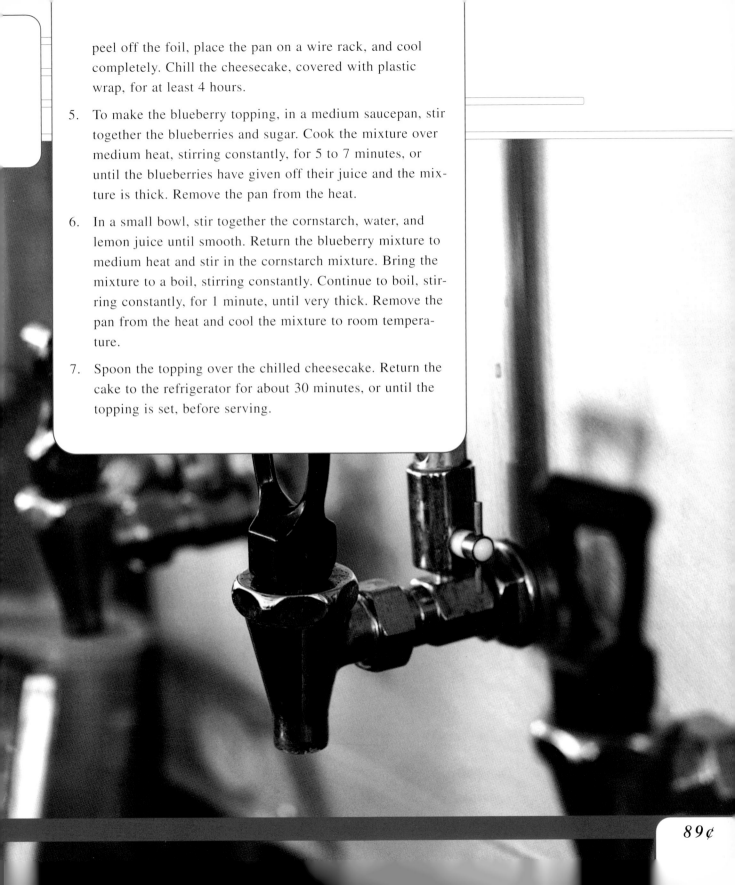

peel off the foil, place the pan on a wire rack, and cool completely. Chill the cheesecake, covered with plastic wrap, for at least 4 hours.

5. To make the blueberry topping, in a medium saucepan, stir together the blueberries and sugar. Cook the mixture over medium heat, stirring constantly, for 5 to 7 minutes, or until the blueberries have given off their juice and the mixture is thick. Remove the pan from the heat.

6. In a small bowl, stir together the cornstarch, water, and lemon juice until smooth. Return the blueberry mixture to medium heat and stir in the cornstarch mixture. Bring the mixture to a boil, stirring constantly. Continue to boil, stirring constantly, for 1 minute, until very thick. Remove the pan from the heat and cool the mixture to room temperature.

7. Spoon the topping over the chilled cheesecake. Return the cake to the refrigerator for about 30 minutes, or until the topping is set, before serving.

89¢

Chocolate Marble Cheesecake

CHOCOLATE CRUMB CRUST

1¼ cups chocolate wafer cookie crumbs

3 tablespoons unsalted butter, melted

CHEESECAKE FILLING

7 ounces semisweet or bittersweet
    chocolate, chopped

5 tablespoons water

2 pounds cream cheese, softened

1¼ cups granulated sugar

4 large eggs

1 tablespoon cornstarch

2 teaspoons vanilla extract

¼ teaspoon salt

2½ cups sour cream

This dramatic cheesecake, with swirls of chocolate throughout, boasts a chocolate-charged cookie crust. For a down-home diner taste, use a domestic semisweet chocolate in the filling. For a more sophisticated cake, use an imported high-end bittersweet chocolate.

1. To make the crumb crust, preheat the oven to 350°F. Butter the bottom and sides of a 9-inch springform pan. Stir together the cookie crumbs and butter until well combined. Pat the crumb mixture onto the bottom of the prepared pan in an even layer. Refrigerate the crust while you make the filling.

2. To make the cheesecake filling, place the chocolate and water in the top of a double boiler over barely simmering water and heat, stirring occasionally, until completely melted. Remove the pan from the heat, separate the top pan from the bottom, and let the chocolate cool until tepid.

3. In an electric mixer, using the paddle attachment or beaters, beat the cream cheese and sugar on medium-low speed until smooth and creamy, about 2 minutes. Add the eggs, one at a time, beating well after each addition and stopping to scrape down the sides of the bowl as necessary. Beat in the cornstarch, vanilla, and salt. Beat in the sour cream on low speed, mixing just until blended.

4. Gently whisk about 1¼ cups of the cheesecake batter into the tepid chocolate mixture. Pour the remaining plain cheesecake batter into the prepared pan. Spoon the chocolate batter over the plain batter, covering the other layer almost completely. Using a small rubber spatula, gently

swirl the two batters together by pulling the plain batter up from the bottom. Do this 10 to 12 times, taking care not to touch the bottom of the pan.

5. Bake the cake for 20 minutes. Reduce the oven temperature to 225°F and bake for 1½ hours longer, or until the center no longer looks wet. Turn the oven off (without opening the door) and leave the cake in the closed oven for an additional hour. Refrigerate the cake for at least 4 hours, or overnight, before serving.

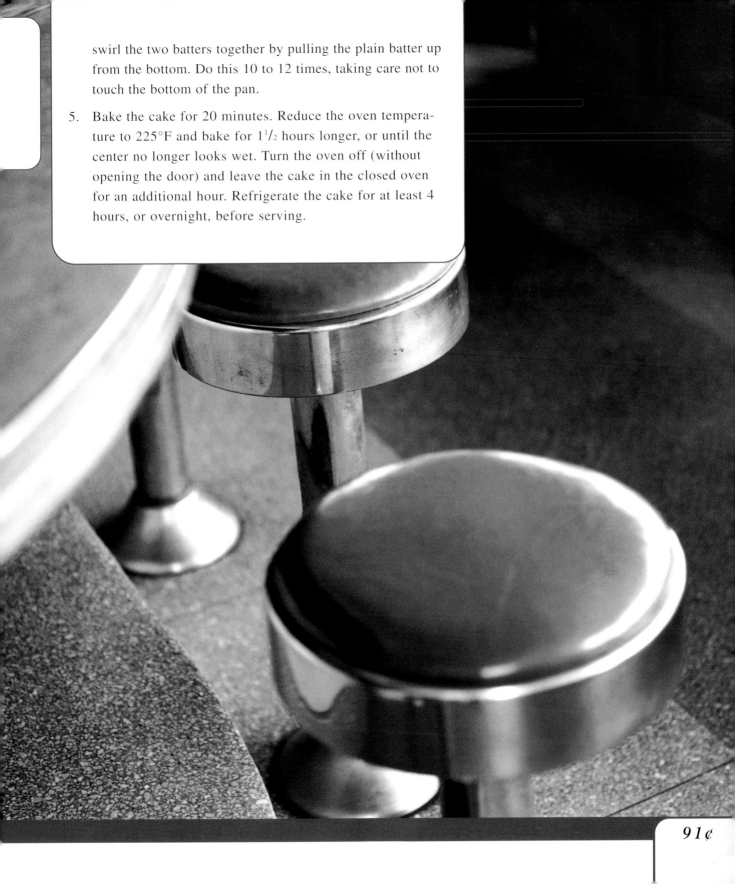

91¢

Turtle Cheesecake

CHEESECAKE FILLING

$1/3$ cup graham cracker crumbs

$1^3/4$ pounds cream cheese, softened

$1^1/2$ cups granulated sugar

2 tablespoons cornstarch, sifted

$1/2$ cup sour cream

4 large eggs

$2/3$ cup heavy cream

1 tablespoon vanilla extract

CARAMEL TOPPING

$1/2$ cup heavy cream

1 cup granulated sugar

$1/2$ cup water

2 tablespoons unsalted butter

1 teaspoon vanilla extract

PECAN GARNISH

$1/2$ cup pecan pieces, toasted (page 26)

CHOCOLATE DRIZZLE

2 ounces semisweet chocolate, chopped

$1/4$ cup heavy cream

Marshall Rosenthal is a Reno-based pastry chef who grew up in Baltimore. Every Sunday when he was a child, his parents took him to the Double-T Diner in Baltimore for ham steak, eggs over-easy, and hot buttermilk biscuits. For dessert, there was a large selection of cheesecakes. Here is Marshall's recipe for his favorite variety, based on the famous Midwestern candy that irresistibly combines caramel, chocolate, and pecans.

1. To make the cheesecake filling, preheat the oven to 350°F. Butter the bottom and sides of a 9-inch springform pan. Dust the pan with the graham cracker crumbs and tap out the excess.

2. In an electric mixer, using the paddle attachment or beaters, beat the cream cheese and the sugar on medium speed until smooth and creamy, about 2 minutes. Add the cornstarch and mix until combined. Add the sour cream and mix on low speed just until combined. Add the eggs, one at a time, beating well after each addition and scraping down the sides of the bowl as necessary. Add the heavy cream and vanilla and mix until blended.

3. Scrape the batter into the prepared pan. Bake the cake for 30 minutes. Reduce the oven temperature to 225°F and bake an additional 60 to 70 minutes, or just until the center no longer looks wet. Turn the oven off (without opening the door) and leave the cake in the closed oven for an additional hour. Remove the cake from the oven and cool on a wire rack for 30 minutes. Refrigerate the cheesecake for at least 3 hours before making the topping.

4. To make the caramel topping, measure out the heavy cream and have it ready near the stove. In a small, heavy saucepan, combine the sugar and water and bring to a boil over medium-high heat, stirring to dissolve the sugar. Increase the heat to high and cook the mixture for 8 to 10 minutes, or until it turns a dark amber. Remove the pan from the heat and gradually stir in the heavy cream (the mixture will bubble vigorously). Return the pan to medium heat and stir just until smooth. Remove the pan from the heat and stir in the butter until completely melted. Stir in the vanilla extract. Scrape the topping into a medium bowl and refrigerate for 1 hour, or until it is a spreadable consistency.

5. Remove the side of the springform pan from the cake. Using a small offset metal spatula, spread the caramel topping over the top and sides of the cheesecake, covering it completely. Press the toasted pecans around the side of the cake. Refrigerate the cake while you make the chocolate drizzle.

6. To make the chocolate drizzle, place the chocolate in the top of a double boiler over barely simmering water and heat, stirring occasionally, until completely melted. Slowly whisk in the heavy cream until smooth. Remove the pan from the heat and separate the top pan from the bottom. Let the chocolate mixture cool for 10 to 15 minutes, or until it is just warm.

7. Scrape the chocolate into a small, sealable plastic bag and seal the bag. Cut a very small hole in one of the bottom corners of the bag (better to cut a hole too small than too large). Drizzle the top of the cake with the chocolate mixture, using it all. Refrigerate the cake for at least 1 hour before serving.

CHAPTER 7

Cobblers, Crisps, and Other Fruit Favorites

Cousins of the fruit pie, these desserts are made from a generous jumble of fruit combined with buttery dough or streusel topping. They are down-home desserts, well-loved as diner specials. Since these desserts do not travel well, diner owners generally do not buy them from outside sources. They are baked on the premises, during the season of the fruit featured in the dessert, and served warm with a scoop of ice cream or dollop of whipped cream. As warm and inviting as diners themselves, these simple desserts evoke feelings of home, whether eaten on the road at a diner counter or at your own kitchen table.

Although they are similar to pies, these desserts require less work and technical skill. They can be assembled ahead (or partly assembled, in the case of the strawberry shortcakes) and baked or heated up shortly before serving. Make one of these desserts when you're short on time but still want to serve something freshly baked and wonderful.

Apple-Raspberry Crisp with Pecan Crunch Topping

Makes 8 servings

PECAN TOPPING

$^1/_2$ cup all-purpose flour

$^1/_2$ cup firmly packed light brown sugar

1 teaspoon ground cinnamon

$^1/_8$ teaspoon salt

6 tablespoons ($^3/_4$ stick) chilled unsalted
   butter, cut into $^1/_2$-inch cubes

$^1/_2$ cup pecan halves

FRUIT FILLING

$2^1/_2$ pounds Golden Delicious apples
   (6 or 7 medium apples), peeled,
   cored, and thinly sliced

1 tablespoon fresh lemon juice

$^1/_2$ cup granulated sugar

2 tablespoons all-purpose flour

$^1/_2$ teaspoon ground cinnamon

3 tablespoons applejack

3 tablespoons unsalted butter, cut into
   $^1/_4$-inch cubes

$1^1/_2$ cups fresh or frozen raspberries
   (not in syrup)

Raspberries add a dash of color and tartness to this deliciously simple apple crisp, while pecans deliver crunch to the fragrant topping. Although the addition of applejack to the filling is outside the diner world, it punches up the apple flavor and gives the filling a nice kick. Make this dessert on a chilly autumn day, and serve it warm with vanilla ice cream or whipped cream.

1. To make the pecan topping, place the flour, brown sugar, cinnamon, and salt in a food processor and pulse until combined. Add the butter pieces and pulse a few times, just until the mixture resembles coarse meal. Add the pecans and pulse just until they are coarsely chopped.

2. Preheat the oven to 350°F. Butter the bottom and sides of a 9-by-13-inch glass baking dish.

3. To make the fruit filling, in a large bowl, toss the apple slices with the lemon juice. Add the granulated sugar, flour, and cinnamon and stir to combine. Add the apple brandy and butter cubes and toss until combined. Gently toss in the raspberries. Evenly spread the apple mixture in the prepared pan. Sprinkle the pecan topping evenly over the filling.

4. Bake the crisp for 40 minutes, or until the fruit is bubbling and the top is browned. Serve warm.

96¢

CHAPTER 7: COBBLERS, CRISPS, AND OTHER FRUIT FAVORITES

Ginger Peachy Cobbler

This cobbler, a version of the classic peach cobbler served in diners during peach season, combines juicy sliced peaches and spicy ginger in a delicious filling enriched with a small amount of cream. The topping is made from light, flaky biscuits flavored with flecks of crystallized ginger. This recipe is also wonderful with nectarines in place of the peaches.

FRUIT FILLING

3 pounds ripe peaches (about 6 large peaches)

$2/3$ cup granulated sugar

2 tablespoons all-purpose flour

1 teaspoon peeled and grated fresh ginger

$1/2$ teaspoon ground cinnamon

1 tablespoon fresh lemon juice

1 tablespoon heavy cream

BISCUIT TOPPING

$1^1/4$ cups all-purpose flour

$1/4$ cup granulated sugar

1 teaspoon baking powder

$1/4$ teaspoon ground ginger

$1/4$ teaspoon salt

6 tablespoons ($3/4$ stick) chilled unsalted butter, cut into $1/2$-inch cubes

1 teaspoon vanilla extract

$1/2$ cup plus 1 tablespoon heavy cream

1 tablespoon finely chopped crystallized ginger

1. Preheat the oven to 375°F. Butter the bottom and sides of a 9-by-13-inch glass baking dish.

2. To make the fruit filling, blanch the peaches by plunging them into boiling water for 30 seconds. Remove them to a bowl of ice water and, using your hands, slip off the skins. Cut into $1/4$-inch-thick slices off the pit, and place the slices in a large bowl.

3. In a small bowl, stir together the sugar, flour, fresh ginger, cinnamon, lemon juice, and cream. Pour the mixture over the peach slices and toss to coat. Transfer the fruit to the prepared baking dish.

4. To make the biscuit topping, place the flour, sugar, baking powder, ground ginger, and salt in a food processor and pulse until combined. Add the butter pieces and process until the mixture resembles coarse meal. Stir the vanilla into $1/2$ cup of the cream and add to the flour mixture. Pulse just until the dough starts to hold together.

5. Scrape the dough onto a lightly floured piece of waxed paper and shape it into a disk. Roll the dough out ¼ inch thick. Using a 2-inch round fluted biscuit cutter, cut out as many biscuits as possible. Gather up the scraps, reroll them, and cut out more biscuits, until you have a total of 12. Arrange the biscuits on top of the fruit filling, spacing them evenly. Brush the biscuits with the remaining 1 table-spoon heavy cream and sprinkle them with the crystallized ginger.

6. Bake the cobbler for 40 minutes, or until the fruit is bubbling and the biscuits are golden brown. Serve warm.

Cherry-Almond Oat Crumble

ALMOND CRUMBLE TOPPING

6 tablespoons ($^3/_4$ stick) unsalted butter, slightly softened

$^1/_2$ cup firmly packed light brown sugar

$^1/_4$ cup almond paste

$^1/_2$ teaspoon grated lemon zest

$^3/_4$ cup all-purpose flour

$^1/_4$ teaspoon salt

$^1/_2$ cup old-fashioned rolled oats

$^1/_2$ cup coarsely chopped blanched almonds

FRUIT FILLING

2 cans (16 ounces each) sweet, dark cherries in syrup

2 tablespoons cornstarch

$^1/_4$ cup granulated sugar

1 teaspoon fresh lemon juice

$^1/_4$ teaspoon ground cinnamon

$^1/_4$ teaspoon almond extract

Pinch of salt

2 tablespoons chilled unsalted butter, cut into $^1/_4$-inch cubes

Sweet cherries and almonds are at the heart of this crumble (another word for crisp), with a boost in almond flavor from the addition of almond paste and almond extract in the topping. Dish it out while it's still warm, and top each serving with a scoop of vanilla ice cream, à la the local diner.

1. Preheat the oven to 375°F. Butter the bottom and sides of a 2-quart shallow baking dish.

2. To make the almond crumble topping, in an electric mixer, using the paddle attachment or beaters, beat together the butter, sugar, almond paste, and lemon zest on medium speed until smooth, about 2 minutes. With the mixer on low speed, gradually add the flour and salt and mix just until crumbly. Stir in the oats and almonds. Set the topping aside while you prepare the fruit filling.

3. To make the fruit filling, drain the cherries, reserving the syrup. In a medium bowl, combine the cornstarch with 2 tablespoons of the syrup, stirring until all the lumps disappear. Add the remaining syrup, stirring to combine. Whisk in the sugar, lemon juice, cinnamon, almond extract, and salt. Add the cherries, tossing to coat them evenly with the syrup mixture. Pour the filling into the prepared baking dish. Scatter the butter pieces over the filling. Sprinkle the crumble topping evenly over the fruit.

4. Bake the crumble for 30 to 35 minutes, or until the top is golden and the fruit is bubbling. Serve warm.

Black-and-Blue Cornmeal Cobbler

FRUIT FILLING

2 cups blueberries

2 cups blackberries

$3/4$ cup granulated sugar

1 tablespoon cornstarch

$1/2$ teaspoon ground cinnamon

2 teaspoons fresh lemon juice

$1/2$ teaspoon grated lemon zest

2 tablespoons unsalted butter, melted

CORNMEAL BISCUIT TOPPING

$3/4$ cup all-purpose flour

$1/4$ cup yellow cornmeal

2 tablespoons granulated sugar

$3/4$ teaspoon baking powder

$1/4$ teaspoon baking soda

$1/4$ teaspoon ground cinnamon

$1/4$ teaspoon salt

3 tablespoons chilled unsalted butter,
cut into $1/4$-inch cubes

6 tablespoons buttermilk

Whole milk, for glazing the biscuits

Ripe blackberries and blueberries are baked together with a yellow cornmeal biscuit topping in this flavorful cobbler. Serve it warm with vanilla or lemon ice cream or sweetened whipped cream.

1. Preheat the oven to 400°F. Butter the bottom and sides of a $1^1/_2$-quart shallow baking dish.

2. To make the fruit filling, in a medium bowl, combine the berries, sugar, cornstarch, cinnamon, lemon juice, lemon zest, and butter, tossing well to combine. Pour the filling into the prepared baking dish.

3. Bake the filling for 30 minutes. Remove the dish from the oven and place it on a wire rack. Raise the oven temperature to 425°F.

4. To make the cornmeal biscuit topping, in a medium bowl, gently whisk together the flour, cornmeal, 1 tablespoon of the sugar, the baking powder, baking soda, cinnamon, and salt. Scatter the butter evenly over the flour mixture. Using a pastry blender or 2 knives, cut in the butter until the mixture resembles coarse bread crumbs. Add the buttermilk all at once and stir with a spoon until combined. Gently knead the dough against the sides of the bowl a few times until the dough is smooth and the bowl is clean.

5. Transfer the dough to a lightly floured work surface and pat it into a disk. Roll out the dough $^3/_8$ inch thick. Using a $2^1/_4$-inch round fluted biscuit cutter, cut out as many biscuits as possible. Gather up the scraps, reroll them, and cut out more biscuits until you have a total of 8. Arrange the biscuits on top of the hot fruit filling, spacing them evenly. Brush the top of the biscuits with milk and then sprinkle them with the remaining 1 tablespoon sugar.

6. Bake the cobbler for another 15 minutes, or until the biscuits are puffed and golden brown. Serve warm.

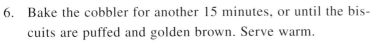

Strawberry Shortcake

STRAWBERRY FILLING

3 pints strawberries, hulled and halved
   lengthwise (or quartered if large)

4 to 5 tablespoons granulated sugar

1 teaspoon grated lemon zest

WHIPPED CREAM

2 cups heavy cream

$^1/_4$ cup granulated sugar

2 teaspoons vanilla extract

1 teaspoon finely grated lemon zest

SHORTCAKES

1 cup all-purpose flour

1 cup cake flour

$^1/_4$ cup granulated sugar

2$^1/_2$ teaspoons baking powder

$^1/_2$ teaspoon salt

6 tablespoons ($^3/_4$ stick) chilled unsalted
   butter, cut into $^1/_4$-inch cubes

$^3/_4$ cup plus 1 tablespoon heavy cream or
   half-and-half

Here is a diner classic: tender, buttery biscuits topped with sweet, juicy strawberries and lots of softly whipped cream. I've added a little lemon to the berries and whipped cream to bring out the berry flavor. Assemble the shortcakes just before serving, so they don't get soft and soggy.

1. To make the strawberry filling, place the berries in a bowl and toss them with the sugar (if they are sweet, use 4 tablespoons; if they are slightly tart, use 5 tablespoons) and lemon zest. Cover and refrigerate the berries for at least 4 to 6 hours, or until they have released their juices.

2. To make the whipped cream, in an electric mixer, using the whisk attachment or beaters, beat the cream on medium-low speed for 30 seconds. Increase the speed to medium-high and add the sugar, vanilla, and lemon zest. Beat until the cream forms soft peaks. Cover and refrigerate until ready to assemble the desserts.

3. To make the shortcakes, preheat the oven to 400°F. In a large bowl, stir together the flours, 3 tablespoons of the sugar, the baking powder, and the salt with a whisk. Scatter the butter evenly over the flour mixture. Using a pastry blender or 2 knives, cut in the butter until it is the size of small peas. Add $^3/_4$ cup of the cream or half-and-half and stir just until the mixture forms a soft dough. Do not over-mix. With a lightly floured hand, gather the dough into a shaggy ball and gently knead the dough 5 or 6 times against the sides of the bowl until almost smooth.

4. Transfer the dough to a lightly floured work surface. Roll the dough out $^1/_2$ inch thick. Using a 3$^1/_2$-inch round biscuit

cutter, cut out 3 shortcakes and place them on an ungreased baking sheet. Gather up the scraps and pat them into a flat disk. Roll and cut out 2 more shortcakes and place them on the sheet. Repeat to form 1 more shortcake. Brush the shortcakes with the remaining 1 tablespoon heavy cream or half-and-half, and sprinkle them with the remaining 1 tablespoon sugar.

5. Bake the shortcakes for 15 to 17 minutes, or until light golden brown. Cool them for a few minutes on the baking sheet.

6. To assemble the strawberry shortcakes, using a serrated knife or a fork, split the shortcakes in half horizontally. Spoon some of the strawberry juice over the cut side of each bottom half. Divide the filling among the shortcakes, spooning it over the bottom halves. Top the filling with a large dollop of the whipped cream. Set each shortcake top on the whipped cream, placing it slightly off center. Serve the shortcakes immediately, placing any remaining whipped cream in a bowl alongside the desserts.

CHAPTER 8

Proof of the Pudding

Puddings are what childhood memories are made of. When I was a girl, my first choice for dessert when our family went to the diner was chocolate pudding, served in a sundae glass, with lots of whipped cream (my sister liked it with heavy cream poured on top). While waiting for a booth, we'd eye the pudding selection in the refrigerated glass case. There was rice, chocolate, vanilla, and butterscotch. At home, after school, we'd try to re-create the diner's pudding, using a boxed mix. It never occurred to us that there was any other way to make the stuff. We knew it didn't taste as good as the diner pudding but were clueless as to the reason.

Now I know what the cooks at the diner knew all along. Preparing pudding from scratch is not much more time-consuming than making it from a mix. Most of the recipes in this chapter can be made in about 20 minutes, plus time for chilling. I've included two types of pudding: those cooked on top of the stove and those baked in the oven.

For those who appreciate the filmlike skin that forms on top of a chilled pudding, pour it into shallow individual bowls (to maximize the amount of skin) and don't cover with plastic wrap before chilling. Of the two baked puddings in this chapter, the Rich Bread and Butter Pudding is more like a custard with a crisp topping, while the Baked Fudge Pudding is more like a really moist pudding cake. Once you try these puddings, you'll welcome their addition to your dessert repertoire and relish the childhood memories they will undoubtedly conjure up.

Rum-Raisin Rice Pudding

Makes 6 servings

$1/_2$ cup golden raisins

$1/_4$ cup Myers's dark rum

$2^3/_4$ cups whole milk

1 cup long-grain white rice

$1/_2$ cup firmly packed light brown sugar

$1/_2$ cup granulated sugar

2 tablespoons unsalted butter

1 teaspoon salt

$1/_4$ teaspoon ground cinnamon

$1^1/_2$ cups half-and-half

1 tablespoon cornstarch

3 large egg yolks, lightly beaten

$1^1/_2$ teaspoons vanilla extract

In Europe, rice has long been an ingredient used in fancy molded desserts, such as riz à l'impératrice. *In America, rice pudding has always been pure home-style comfort food, available at nearly every diner. In this version, the rice is slowly cooked to creamy perfection. Rum-soaked raisins and brown sugar add a dark, sweet flavor.*

1. In a small saucepan, combine the raisins and rum. Bring to a boil over medium-high heat. Remove the pan from the heat and let steep while you make the pudding.

2. In a medium, heavy saucepan, combine the milk, rice, brown sugar, granulated sugar, butter, salt, cinnamon, and 1 cup of the half-and-half. Cook over medium heat until the milk mixture comes to a gentle boil. Stir the mixture, cover the pan, and reduce the heat to low. Cook for 40 to 45 minutes, or until the rice is cooked through and much of the liquid is absorbed.

3. In a small bowl, place the cornstarch. Gradually whisk in the remaining $1/_2$ cup half-and-half until smooth. Whisk in the egg yolks. Whisk about $1/_2$ cup of the hot rice mixture into the yolk mixture. Return this mixture to the pudding in the saucepan. Cook over medium heat, stirring constantly, until the mixture just starts to bubble. Continue to cook, stirring, for 1 minute, or until the mixture thickens slightly. Remove the pan from the heat.

4. Add the vanilla to the rum-raisin mixture, and stir the mixture into the rice pudding. Divide the pudding among 6 sundae glasses, cover with plastic wrap (unless you want a skin to form), pressing it directly onto the surface of the pudding, and refrigerate for about 2 hours, or until well chilled.

$1.08

CHAPTER 8: *PROOF OF THE PUDDING*

Creamy Tapioca Pudding

Tapioca pudding, like rice pudding, is true diner food. Ground from the root of the cassava plant, tapioca is a starchy substance with a subtle taste and pearly texture. This pudding, sweetened with condensed milk and enriched with egg yolk, is as simple to make as it is satisfying to eat. Garnish with whipped cream and a sprinkle of cinnamon, if you like.

$1/3$ cup quick-cooking tapioca

$2^1/_2$ cups whole milk

1 can (14 ounces) sweetened
   condensed milk

1 large whole egg

1 large egg yolk

1 teaspoon vanilla extract

$1/4$ teaspoon salt

1. In a large saucepan, combine the tapioca and whole milk. Allow to stand for 10 minutes.

2. Stir in the sweetened condensed milk and cook over medium heat, stirring constantly, until the mixture comes to a simmer. Simmer, stirring, for 2 minutes.

3. In a medium bowl, whisk the whole egg and egg yolk until smooth. Gradually whisk in about 1 cup of the hot milk mixture. Whisk this mixture into the remaining pudding. Cook, stirring constantly, over low heat until the pudding starts to thicken, about 2 minutes. Remove the pan from the heat and stir in the vanilla and salt. Allow the pudding to cool in the saucepan for 20 minutes.

4. Spoon the pudding into 6 sundae glasses, cover with plastic wrap (unless you want a skin to form), pressing it directly onto the surface of the pudding, and refrigerate for about 2 hours, or until well chilled.

$1.09

Butterscotch Pudding

$^1/_3$ cup cornstarch

$^1/_2$ cup firmly packed light brown sugar

$^1/_2$ cup firmly packed dark brown sugar

$^1/_2$ teaspoon salt

2 cups whole milk

1 cup half-and-half

3 large egg yolks

3 tablespoons unsalted butter, cut into tablespoons

2 teaspoons vanilla extract

A combination of the subtle flavors of brown sugar and butter, butterscotch works best in simple desserts like puddings and sundaes where it's not overwhelmed by competing tastes. This pudding is true-blue butterscotch, miles above the boxed-mix variety, although not much harder to make. Serve it with whipped cream or heavy cream, poured on top, if desired.

1. In a medium saucepan, stir together the cornstarch, sugars, and salt. Gradually whisk in the milk and half-and-half. Place over medium-high heat and bring to a boil, whisking constantly. Remove the pan from the heat.

2. In a medium bowl, whisk the egg yolks until smooth. Whisk about 1 cup of the hot milk mixture into the yolks. Return this mixture to the saucepan and cook over medium heat, whisking constantly, until the mixture comes to a gentle boil. Continue to boil, whisking constantly, for 1 minute. Immediately remove the pan from the heat and whisk in the butter pieces until they are completely melted. Whisk in the vanilla. Cover the pudding with waxed paper and cool to room temperature.

3. Spoon the pudding into 6 sundae glasses, cover with plastic wrap (unless you want a skin to form), pressing it directly onto the surface of the pudding, and refrigerate for about 2 hours, or until well chilled.

Chocolate Malt Pudding

Rich, chocolaty, and creamy, this pudding gets a sweet malt finish from the addition of barley malt syrup. Serve the pudding in a tall sundae glass with a long spoon.

$1/2$ cup granulated sugar

$1/4$ cup cornstarch

$1/8$ teaspoon salt

$1^3/_4$ cups whole milk

1 cup heavy cream

$1/4$ cup barley malt syrup

3 large egg yolks

2 ounces semisweet chocolate, coarsely chopped

2 tablespoons unsalted butter, cut into tablespoons

1 teaspoon vanilla extract

Sweetened whipped cream, for garnish

1. In a medium saucepan, stir together the sugar, cornstarch, and salt. Gradually whisk in the milk, cream, and barley malt syrup. Place the saucepan over medium heat and bring to a boil, whisking constantly. Remove the pan from the heat.

2. In a medium bowl, whisk the egg yolks until smooth. Whisk about 1 cup of the hot milk mixture into the yolks. Return this mixture to the saucepan and cook over medium heat, whisking constantly, until the mixture comes to a gentle boil. Continue to boil, whisking constantly, for 1 minute. Immediately remove the pan from the heat and whisk in the chopped chocolate and butter until they are completely melted. Whisk in the vanilla.

3. Spoon into 4 serving dishes, cover with plastic wrap (unless you want a skin to form), pressing it directly onto the surface of the pudding, and refrigerate for about 2 hours, or until well chilled. Serve with whipped cream.

Maple Pudding with Sugared Pecans

Makes 4 servings

SUGARED PECANS

1 tablespoon egg white

3 tablespoons granulated sugar

$^1/_2$ teaspoon ground cinnamon

$^3/_4$ cup pecan halves

MAPLE PUDDING

$^1/_4$ cup cornstarch

$^1/_4$ teaspoon salt

$2^1/_2$ cups whole milk

$^1/_2$ cup firmly packed dark brown sugar

$^1/_2$ cup pure maple syrup

3 large egg yolks

3 tablespoons unsalted butter, cut into tablespoons

2 teaspoons vanilla extract

$^1/_2$ teaspoon maple flavoring

Sweetened whipped cream, for garnish

Pure maple flavor and the crunch of sugared pecans make this pudding one of my favorites. The sugared pecans can be used as a garnish for other desserts, too, such as Southern Sweet Potato Spice Pie (page 49) or Carrot Cake (page 62).

1. To make the sugared pecans, preheat the oven to 350°F. In a small bowl, whisk together the egg white, granulated sugar, and cinnamon until well blended. Add the pecan halves and toss with a spoon until the pecans are completely coated with the egg white–sugar mixture. Spread the coated pecans on a baking sheet.

2. Bake, tossing occasionally, for 10 to 12 minutes, or until fragrant. Transfer the baking sheet to a wire rack and cool the nuts completely. Chop the nuts coarsely and set aside.

3. To make the maple pudding, in a medium nonreactive saucepan, whisk together the cornstarch, salt, milk, brown sugar, and maple syrup until smooth. Place the saucepan over medium heat and bring to a gentle boil, whisking constantly. Remove the pan from the heat.

4. In a medium bowl, whisk the yolks until smooth. Whisk about 1 cup of the hot milk mixture into the yolks. Return this mixture to the saucepan and cook over medium heat, whisking constantly, until the mixture comes to a boil. Continue to boil, whisking constantly, for 1 minute. Remove the pan from the heat and whisk in the butter pieces until completely melted. Whisk in the vanilla, maple flavoring, and $^1/_2$ cup of the chopped pecans.

$1.12

5. Spoon into 4 sundae glasses, cover with plastic wrap (unless you want a skin to form), pressing it directly onto the surface of the pudding, and refrigerate for about 2 hours, or until well chilled. Just before serving, garnish with whipped cream and the reserved sugared pecans.

Banana Caramel Pudding

PUDDING

$^3/_4$ cup granulated sugar

$^1/_4$ cup water

$^1/_2$ cup heavy cream

3 tablespoons plus 1 teaspoon cornstarch

2 cups whole milk

Pinch of salt

2 large egg yolks

2 tablespoons unsalted butter, cut into tablespoons

2 teaspoons vanilla extract

1 medium banana

12 vanilla wafers

GARNISH

1 small banana

Sweetened whipped cream

4 vanilla wafers

Banana pudding is a layered dessert, similar to an English trifle. Extremely popular down South, it also is frequently showcased on diner menus throughout the country. This recipe features a caramel pudding layered with bananas and vanilla wafer cookies. The wafers soften as they absorb the pudding, and become almost like a thin layer of sponge cake.

1. In a medium saucepan, stir together the sugar and water. Cook over medium heat, stirring occasionally, until the sugar dissolves. Increase the heat to high and, without stirring, cook the mixture until it turns a golden amber. Remove the pan from the heat and carefully add a few tablespoons of the heavy cream (the mixture will bubble up). Gradually add the remaining heavy cream.

2. In a small bowl, whisk together the cornstarch and $^1/_4$ cup of the milk until smooth. Whisk the cornstarch mixture and the remaining $1^3/_4$ cups milk into the caramel mixture in the saucepan. Stir in the salt. Place over medium heat and cook, whisking constantly, until the mixture comes to a boil (any hardened bits of caramel will dissolve as the mixture boils). Remove the pan from the heat.

3. In a medium bowl, whisk the egg yolks until smooth. Whisk about 1 cup of the hot caramel mixture into the yolks. Return this mixture to the saucepan and cook over medium heat, whisking constantly, until the mixture comes to a boil. Continue to boil, whisking constantly, for 1 minute. Immediately remove the pan from the heat and whisk in the butter until completely melted. Whisk in the vanilla. Strain the pudding through a fine-mesh sieve into a medium bowl.

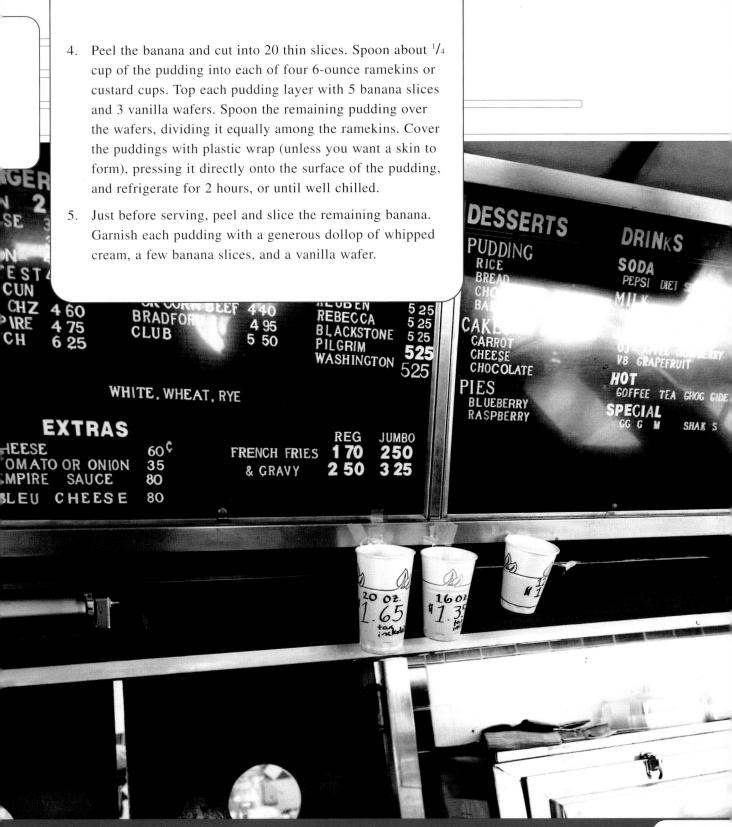

4. Peel the banana and cut into 20 thin slices. Spoon about ¼ cup of the pudding into each of four 6-ounce ramekins or custard cups. Top each pudding layer with 5 banana slices and 3 vanilla wafers. Spoon the remaining pudding over the wafers, dividing it equally among the ramekins. Cover the puddings with plastic wrap (unless you want a skin to form), pressing it directly onto the surface of the pudding, and refrigerate for 2 hours, or until well chilled.

5. Just before serving, peel and slice the remaining banana. Garnish each pudding with a generous dollop of whipped cream, a few banana slices, and a vanilla wafer.

Rich Bread-and-Butter Pudding

12 slices (¹/₄ inch thick) fresh French bread

¹/₄ cup (¹/₂ stick) unsalted butter, softened

¹/₄ teaspoon ground cinnamon

2 cups whole milk

2 cups heavy cream

1 cup granulated sugar

4 large eggs

2 large egg yolks

¹/₄ teaspoon freshly grated nutmeg

¹/₈ teaspoon salt

2 teaspoons vanilla extract

¹/₄ cup coarsely chopped walnuts

Confectioners' sugar, for dusting

Once considered old-fashioned, bread pudding has recently made a big comeback on restaurant dessert menus. It has always, however, had a prominent place on the diner counter. This version used fresh French bread, which is toasted and then spread with cinnamon-butter. The custard is rich in eggs, milk, and cream, and because it is baked in a water bath, remains perfectly smooth. Walnuts and confectioners' sugar add a pretty finish.

1. Butter the bottom and sides of a shallow 2-quart glass baking dish.

2. Preheat the oven to 350°F. Place the bread slices on a baking sheet and bake for about 5 minutes, or until the bread is almost crisp but not browned. Remove the sheet from the oven and allow the bread to cool completely. Leave the oven on.

3. In a small bowl, using a rubber spatula, combine the butter with the cinnamon. Spread this mixture evenly over one side of each bread slice, using the entire mixture. Arrange the bread slices, buttered side up, in the prepared baking dish.

4. Place the milk, cream, and ¹/₂ cup of the sugar in a medium saucepan and cook over medium heat, stirring occasionally, until the mixture comes to a gentle boil. Remove the pan from the heat and set aside.

5. In a medium bowl, whisk together the whole eggs, egg yolks, and the remaining ¹/₂ cup granulated sugar until well blended. Gradually whisk in the hot cream mixture. Whisk in the nutmeg, salt, and vanilla. Pour the custard mixture

evenly over the bread slices in the baking dish, then press down on the slices to make sure they are saturated. Sprinkle with the chopped nuts.

6. Place the baking dish in a large roasting pan and place it on the oven rack. Pour enough hot water into the roasting pan to reach halfway up the sides of the baking dish. Bake the pudding for 50 minutes, or until golden brown and just set. Serve the pudding warm, dusted with confectioners' sugar.

Baked Fudge Pudding

CHOCOLATE SYRUP

³/₄ cup water

¹/₂ teaspoon instant espresso powder

2 tablespoons unsalted butter, cut into tablespoons

¹/₂ cup firmly packed light brown sugar

¹/₂ ounce semisweet chocolate, chopped

1 teaspoon vanilla extract

PUDDING

1 ounce semisweet chocolate, coarsely chopped

1 tablespoon unsalted butter

¹/₄ cup firmly packed light brown sugar

²/₃ cup cake flour

1 teaspoon baking powder

¹/₈ teaspoon salt

¹/₄ cup miniature semisweet chocolate morsels

¹/₄ cup chopped walnuts

¹/₃ cup buttermilk

BROWN SUGAR WHIPPED CREAM

²/₃ cup heavy cream

1 tablespoon light brown sugar

¹/₂ teaspoon vanilla extract

Baked pudding made with fruit is a familiar diner dessert. This version is all chocolate and combines chocolate buttermilk cake batter with a coffee-tinged chocolate syrup. Studded with chocolate chips and walnuts, it makes a wonderful warm, moist pudding. Generously topped with brown sugar whipped cream, this dessert is indulgent, yet simple.

1. Preheat the oven to 350°F. To make the chocolate syrup, in a medium saucepan, combine the water, espresso powder, butter, and sugar. Place over medium-high heat and cook, stirring constantly, until the sugar is dissolved and the mixture comes to a boil. Remove the pan from the heat and stir in the chocolate until it is completely melted. Stir in the vanilla. Transfer the syrup to a heatproof glass measuring cup.

2. To make the pudding, in the same saucepan used to make the syrup, place the semisweet chocolate and butter. Cook over low heat, stirring constantly, until the chocolate is melted and the mixture is smooth. Remove the pan from the heat and cool slightly.

3. In a medium bowl, combine the brown sugar, cake flour, baking powder, salt, chocolate morsels, and walnuts. Stir in the buttermilk and the chocolate mixture just until combined.

4. Pour about ¹/₄ cup of the chocolate syrup into each of four 8-ounce ramekins or custard cups. One tablespoon at a time, drop 3 rounded tablespoons of the pudding batter into each ramekin. Place the ramekins on a baking sheet and bake for 20 to 25 minutes, or until puffed and bubbling.

5. To make the brown sugar whipped cream, in a medium bowl using a handheld electric mixer, beat the cream, brown sugar, and vanilla until stiff peaks form.

6. Serve each pudding warm with a generous dollop of the whipped cream.

CHAPTER 9

Coffee Break—Cookies, Bars, and Brownies

The urge for a freshly baked chocolate chip cookie, cheesecake bar, or brownie draws some people to a bakery or café. But others head for the local diner, where these portable sweets are displayed on the lunch counter under glass domes. The casual atmosphere and speedy service of the diner encourage anyone hungry and in a hurry to pause for a quick pick-me-up. Kids on their way home from school might stop for a jumbo cookie and a milk shake. Office workers may take a midmorning or afternoon break of coffee and a brownie. And after a quick lunch, when a large dessert won't do, a cookie or brownie rounds out a meal nicely.

Diner cookies, bars, and brownies are never subtle or dainty. The baked goods in this chapter are big and flavorful. Some are thickly frosted, while others are packed with add-ins like chocolate morsels and nuts. All are easily transportable and, wrapped individually, tuck nicely into a lunch box or purse. Store these sweets as directed in each recipe to preserve their flavor and extend their shelf life.

Old-time Peanut Butter Cookies

2½ cups all-purpose flour

2 teaspoons baking powder

½ teaspoon baking soda

¼ teaspoon salt

1 cup (2 sticks) unsalted butter, softened

1 cup creamy peanut butter (not the all-natural kind), at room temperature

1 cup granulated sugar

1 cup firmly packed dark brown sugar

2 large eggs

1 tablespoon vanilla extract

¾ cup chopped unsalted roasted peanuts

These intensely peanutty cookies are slightly crispy on the outside and chewy on the inside. I bake them on an insulated cookie sheet, which prevents them from overbrowning on the bottom. If you don't have one, use two heavy-gauge baking sheets stacked on top of each other.

1. In a medium bowl, stir together the flour, baking powder, baking soda, and salt; set aside.

2. In an electric mixer, using the paddle attachment, beat together the butter and peanut butter on medium speed until smooth. Gradually beat in the granulated and brown sugars. Add the eggs, one at a time, beating well after each addition and stopping to scrape down the sides of the bowl as necessary. Beat in the vanilla.

3. On low speed, add the flour mixture and the peanuts and beat until blended. Cover with plastic wrap and refrigerate for 30 to 45 minutes, or until the dough has firmed up.

4. Position two baking racks near the center of the oven, and preheat the oven to 350°F. Lightly grease 2 insulated cookie sheets.

5. Using a ¼-cup ice-cream scoop or cup measure, scoop 6 portions of the chilled dough onto each cookie sheet, spacing them evenly. Use the palm of your hand to flatten each scoop into a 2½-inch round. Using a fork, making a cross-hatch indentation in the center of each cookie. Slide the fork toward the edge of each cookie to continue the indentation to the edge.

6. Bake the cookies, switching the position of the sheets halfway through baking, for 18 to 20 minutes, or until golden around the edges but still soft in the center. Transfer the cookies to a wire rack to cool completely. They will firm up as they cool. Serve the cookies slightly warm or at room temperature.

Mega Oatmeal, Walnut, and Chocolate Chip Cookies

Makes 32 large cookies

1³/₄ cups all-purpose flour

¹/₂ teaspoon baking soda

¹/₄ teaspoon cream of tartar

³/₄ teaspoon salt

¹/₂ cup (1 stick) plus 3 tablespoons unsalted butter, softened

6 tablespoons solid vegetable shortening

1¹/₃ cups firmly packed light brown sugar

¹/₃ cup granulated sugar

1 tablespoon vanilla extract

2 large eggs

1 tablespoon whole milk

2 cups quick-cooking rolled oats

2¹/₂ cups semisweet chocolate morsels

2 cups walnut pieces

The author of several dessert cookbooks, Lisa Yockelson learned from her mother how to track down a good recipe. As a child, she would accompany her mother on car trips, occasionally stopping at a diner for something sweet. Lisa would pick the coconut cake or chocolate cream pie. Mom would choose the lemon meringue pie or devil's food cake. And then, if she liked the dessert, her mom would attempt to pry the recipe from the cook. These oatmeal cookies are a variation on one of her mother's successful attempts. They are chock-full of rolled oats, chips, and nuts. For the very best taste and texture, serve them freshly baked. The dough will keep in the refrigerator for up to 2 days, which means you can have a batch of something sweet in no time.

1. Preheat the oven to 350° F. Line 2 cookie sheets with parchment paper.

2. In a medium bowl, stir together the flour, baking soda, cream of tartar, and salt; set aside.

3. In an electric mixer, using the paddle attachment or beaters, beat together the butter and shortening on low speed for 3 to 4 minutes, or until light and creamy. Add the brown and granulated sugar; beat on medium speed for 1¹/₂ minutes, or until well blended, stopping to scrape down the sides of the bowl as necessary. Beat in the vanilla. Add the eggs, one at a time, beating well after each addition. Add the milk and beat until combined.

4. On low speed, add the flour mixture and beat only until the flour particles are absorbed. Beat in the rolled oats. Using

a sturdy wooden spoon, stir in the chocolate morsels and walnuts. The dough will be thick, dense with chips and nuts, and heavy.

5. Place 3-tablespoon-sized, slightly rounded mounds of dough 3 to $3^1/_2$ inches apart on the prepared cookie sheets. For the best results, form each dough mass into a somewhat thick, craggy, lightly domed mound. There should be 6 mounds on each sheet.

6. Bake the cookies, switching the position of the sheets halfway through baking, for 12 to 13 minutes, or until pale golden in patches here and there around the edges and the tops are softly set. Place each cookie sheet on a wire rack and let stand for 15 to 20 minutes. With a metal spatula, transfer the cookies to a double sheet of waxed paper. Repeat with the remaining dough. Serve the cookies very fresh.

Classic Black and White Cookies

COOKIE BASE

2 cups all-purpose flour

1 teaspoon baking powder

$^1/_2$ teaspoon baking soda

$^1/_8$ teaspoon salt

$^1/_2$ cup (1 stick) unsalted butter, softened

1 cup granulated sugar

1 large egg

2 teaspoons vanilla extract

$^1/_2$ teaspoon finely grated orange zest

$^1/_2$ cup sour cream

WHITE ICING

1 cup confectioners' sugar

$3^1/_2$ tablespoons heavy cream

$^1/_8$ teaspoon vanilla extract

CHOCOLATE GLAZE

3 ounces semisweet chocolate, chopped

$^1/_4$ cup heavy cream

1 tablespoon light corn syrup

This is the number-one choice of New York–area kids who are fortunate enough to have a diner on their way home from school. "Black and Whites" are jumbo sugar cookies iced dramatically with half vanilla and half chocolate glaze. Ubiquitous at lunch counters in and around New York City, they range from dreadful to sublime. This version has a puffy, orange-scented cookie base topped with satiny smooth white and chocolate icing and represents the cream of the black-and-white-cookie crop.

1. Position 2 baking racks near the center of the oven and preheat the oven to 350°F. Butter 2 large baking sheets.

2. To make the cookie base, in a medium bowl, stir together the flour, baking powder, baking soda, and salt with a whisk.

3. In an electric mixer, using the paddle attachment or beaters, beat the butter on medium speed for about 30 seconds, or until creamy. Gradually beat in the granulated sugar, mixing until well combined. Add the egg, vanilla, and orange zest. Scrape down the sides of the bowl and mix until well blended. Add the sour cream in 3 additions alternately with the flour mixture in 3 additions, blending well after each.

4. Using a $^1/_4$-cup ice-cream scoop or cup measure, scoop 14 portions of the dough onto the baking sheets, spacing them 3 inches apart. Use the palm of your hand to flatten each scoop into a $2^1/_2$-inch round.

5. Bake the cookies, switching the position of the sheets halfway through baking, for 15 to 17 minutes, or until just

beginning to turn light golden brown. Place each cookie sheet on a wire rack and let stand for 2 minutes, then transfer the cookies to the rack and cool completely.

6. To make the white icing, in a small bowl, whisk together the confectioners' sugar, heavy cream, and vanilla until smooth.

7. To make the chocolate glaze, place the chocolate, heavy cream, and corn syrup in the top of a double boiler over barely simmering water. Heat, stirring occasionally, until the chocolate melts and the glaze is smooth. Let cool for about 10 minutes, or until tepid.

8. Using a small, offset metal spatula, spread the white icing on half of each cookie. Let set for 10 minutes.

9. Using the spatula, spread the chocolate glaze on the other half of each cookie. Let set at room temperature for at least 45 minutes. Store between layers of waxed paper in a tightly covered container at room temperature for up to 3 days.

Monster Fudge Nut Cookies

12 ounces semisweet chocolate, chopped

6 tablespoons (³/₄ stick) unsalted butter, cut into tablespoons

²/₃ cup all-purpose flour

1 teaspoon baking powder

¹/₄ teaspoon salt

3 large eggs

1 cup granulated sugar

1 tablespoon vanilla extract

12 ounces Hershey's miniature semisweet kisses*

1¹/₂ cups coarsely chopped walnuts

Packed with oversized chocolate chips and walnuts, these jumbo cookies are bursting with fudge flavor. Just don't overbake them. They should be just set on the outside, and still moist on the inside.

1. Position 2 baking racks near the center of the oven and preheat the oven to 350°F. Grease 2 large baking sheets.

2. Place the chopped chocolate and the butter in the top of a double boiler over barely simmering water. Heat, stirring constantly, until the chocolate melts and the mixture is smooth. Remove the top of the double boiler and let the chocolate mixture cool.

3. In a medium bowl, stir together the flour, baking powder, and salt. Set aside.

4. In an electric mixer, using the whisk attachment, beat the eggs on medium speed until blended. Gradually beat in the sugar, then increase the speed to high. Continue beating for about 5 minutes, or until the mixture is thick and light.

5. Stir the vanilla into the cooled chocolate and add to the egg mixture, beating on medium speed until combined. On low speed, beat in the flour mixture, scraping down the sides of the bowl as necessary. Using a wooden spoon, fold in the miniature kisses and nuts. Cover with plastic wrap and chill in the refrigerator for 10 minutes.

6. Using a $\frac{1}{4}$-cup ice-cream scoop or cup measure, drop the batter onto the prepared baking sheets, spacing the mounds 2 inches apart. Bake the cookies, switching the position of the sheets halfway through baking, for 10 to 12 minutes, or until set on the outside, but still slightly moist on the inside. Place each cookie sheet on a wire rack and let stand for 10 minutes, then transfer the cookies to the rack and cool completely. Serve the cookies slightly warm or at room temperature. Store in an airtight container at room temperature for up to 3 days.

*You may substitute 12 ounces semisweet chocolate, cut into $\frac{1}{2}$-inch chunks.

$1.29

Rocky Road Bars

BROWNIE BASE

5 ounces unsweetened chocolate

1 cup (2 sticks) unsalted butter, cut into tablespoons

2 cups granulated sugar

$1/2$ teaspoon salt

2 teaspoons vanilla extract

3 large eggs

1 cup all-purpose flour

$1^1/2$ cups coarsely chopped walnuts

ROCKY ROAD TOPPING

1 cup coarsely chopped walnuts

1 cup milk chocolate–covered English toffee bits, such as Heath bits

1 cup semisweet chocolate morsels

2 cups miniature marshmallows

Rocky road is a purely American concept that shows up in diners as ice cream or dessert bars. Here excess and indulgence are celebrated by piling nuts, Heath bits, marshmallow, and semi-sweet morsels onto a rich brownie base and serving it all in immodest slabs. Great with a gallon or so of milk.

1. Preheat the oven to 350°F. Butter the bottom and sides of a 9-by-13-inch baking pan.

2. To make the brownie base, place the chocolate and butter in the top of a double boiler over barely simmering water. Heat, stirring constantly, until the chocolate melts and the mixture is smooth. Remove the pan from the heat and let the chocolate mixture cool for 10 minutes.

3. Stir the sugar, salt, and vanilla into the chocolate mixture. Stir in the eggs, one at a time, until there is no trace of yolk. Stir in the flour just until blended. Stir in the nuts. Scrape into the prepared pan and smooth the top with a rubber spatula.

4. Bake the brownie base for 30 minutes, or until a toothpick inserted into the center just barely comes out clean. Remove from the oven and leave the oven on.

5. To make the rocky road topping, sprinkle half of the chopped walnuts evenly over the top of the hot brownie base. Sprinkle half of the toffee pieces, half of the semi-sweet morsels, and half of the miniature marshmallows evenly over the nuts. Repeat these layers.

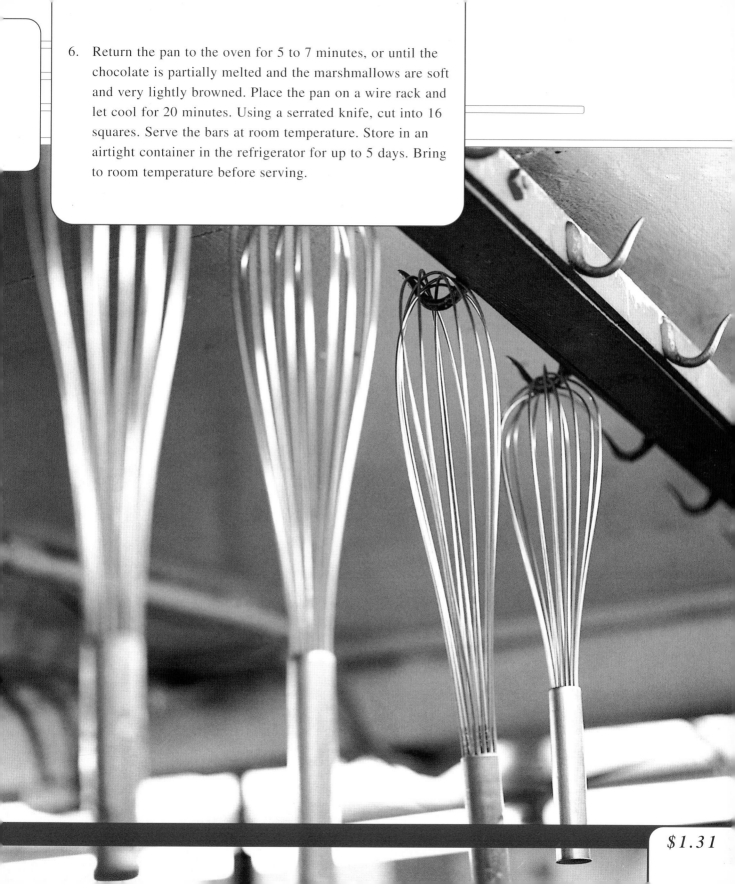

6. Return the pan to the oven for 5 to 7 minutes, or until the chocolate is partially melted and the marshmallows are soft and very lightly browned. Place the pan on a wire rack and let cool for 20 minutes. Using a serrated knife, cut into 16 squares. Serve the bars at room temperature. Store in an airtight container in the refrigerator for up to 5 days. Bring to room temperature before serving.

Chocolate Cheesecake Bars

Makes 12 servings

This is a dense, chewy brownie layer topped with a creamy cheese mixture and lots of pecan halves. The subtle tang of the cheese cuts the richness of the chocolate and the pecans add a nutty crunch.

CHOCOLATE LAYER

6 ounces semisweet chocolate, coarsely chopped

3 ounces unsweetened chocolate, coarsely chopped

1 cup all-purpose flour

$1/4$ teaspoon salt

1 cup (2 sticks) unsalted butter, softened

$1^1/_2$ cups granulated sugar

3 large eggs

1 teaspoon vanilla extract

CHEESECAKE LAYER

1 pound cream cheese, softened

$1/3$ cup granulated sugar

1 large egg

1 tablespoon heavy cream

1 teaspoon vanilla extract

GARNISH

$1/2$ cup pecan pieces

1. Preheat the oven to 300°F. Line a 9-by-13-inch baking pan with aluminum foil so that the foil extends 2 inches beyond the two short ends of the pan. Lightly butter the bottom and sides of the foil-lined pan.

2. To make the chocolate layer, place the semisweet and unsweetened chocolates in the top of a double boiler over barely simmering water. Heat, stirring occasionally, until the chocolates melt. Let cool for about 10 minutes, or until tepid.

3. In a small bowl, stir together the flour and salt with a whisk.

4. In an electric mixer, using the paddle attachment or beaters, beat together the butter and sugar on medium speed for about 1 minute, or until combined. Beat in the eggs, one at a time, beating well after each addition and scraping down the sides of the bowl as necessary. Beat in the melted chocolate and vanilla. On low speed, beat in the flour mixture until blended. Scrape into the prepared pan and smooth the top with a rubber spatula. Place the pan on a flat surface in the freezer for 15 minutes.

$1.32

CHAPTER 9: *COFFEE BREAK—COOKIES, BARS, AND BROWNIES*

5. To make the cheesecake layer, in an electric mixer, using the paddle attachment or beaters, beat together the cream cheese and sugar on medium speed until smooth, about 1 minute. Beat in the egg, cream, and vanilla until smooth. Scrape down the sides of the bowl and beat for another 30 seconds. Scrape the cheese mixture over the chilled chocolate layer and spread it into an even layer. Sprinkle the pecans over the cheese layer.

6. Bake the bars for 70 to 75 minutes, or until a toothpick inserted into the center comes out with a few moist crumbs clinging to it. Do not overbake. Place the pan on a wire rack and cool completely. Using the two ends of the foil as handles, lift the brownies out of the pan. Invert onto a cutting surface and peel off the foil. Reinvert and cut into 3-inch squares. Serve at room temperature. Store in an airtight container in the refrigerator for up to 3 days. Bring to room temperature before serving.

Double-Fudge Frosted Brownies

BROWNIES

$^1/_2$ cup (1 stick) unsalted butter, cut into tablespoons

$^1/_2$ cup lightly packed light brown sugar

6 ounces semisweet chocolate, chopped

2 ounces unsweetened chocolate, chopped

$^3/_4$ cup granulated sugar

3 large eggs

$1^1/_2$ teaspoons vanilla extract

$^1/_2$ cup all-purpose flour

$^1/_4$ teaspoon salt

FROSTING

3 tablespoons unsalted butter, cut into tablespoons

2 ounces unsweetened chocolate

1 ounce milk chocolate

$1^1/_2$ cups confectioners' sugar, sifted

Pinch of salt

$^1/_4$ cup heavy cream

1 teaspoon vanilla extract

GARNISH (OPTIONAL)

$^1/_4$ cup chopped walnuts

Iced brownies are a diner tradition. Moist and chocolaty, these brownies are topped with a satiny chocolate frosting and walnuts. They can be wrapped individually and stored in the refrigerator for up to 5 days or frozen for a month. Bring to room temperature before serving for maximum flavor impact.

1. Preheat the oven to 350°F. Line an 8-inch square baking pan with aluminum foil so that the foil extends 2 inches beyond the two opposite sides of the pan. Lightly butter the bottom and sides of the foil-lined pan.

2. To make the brownies, in a medium saucepan, combine the butter pieces, brown sugar, and semisweet and unsweetened chocolates. Cook over low heat, stirring constantly, until the butter and chocolates melt and the mixture is smooth. Transfer to a medium bowl.

3. With a wooden spoon, stir in the granulated sugar. Stir in the eggs, one at a time, until there is no trace of yolk. Mix in the vanilla. Add the flour and salt and mix vigorously until the mixture is shiny and smooth. Scrape the batter into the prepared pan and smooth the top with a rubber spatula.

4. Bake the brownies for 35 to 40 minutes, or until a toothpick inserted into the center comes out with a few moist crumbs clinging to it. Do not overbake. Place the pan on a wire rack and cool for 45 minutes. Using the two ends of the foil as handles, lift the brownies out of the pan. Invert onto the cooling rack and peel off the foil. Cool completely (the brownies will be frosted on the smooth side).

5. To make the frosting, place the butter and both types of chocolate in a medium saucepan. Heat over very low heat, stirring constantly, until the chocolates melt and the mixture is smooth. Transfer to the bowl of an electric mixer. On low speed, add half of the confectioners' sugar, the salt, and then half of the cream. Blend in the remaining confectioners' sugar and the remaining cream. Beat in the vanilla extract. Beat the frosting on medium speed for 30 seconds, or until smooth and shiny.

6. Spread the frosting over the uncut brownies, making it as smooth as possible. Garnish the top with chopped walnuts, if desired. Cut into 9 squares and serve at room temperature.

CHAPTER 10

Dunkables—Doughnuts, Muffins, and Pastries

Although not strictly thought of as desserts, these breakfast sweets are included because of their popularity in diners. Doughnuts, muffins, and pastries are typical counter fare, to be eaten with, and sometimes dunked into, the ubiquitous cup of coffee.

Doughnuts, popular in the United States since World War I, are small, deep-fried cakes that are leavened by either baking powder or yeast. I've included one of each type here. If you've never made doughnuts before, don't feel daunted by the prospect. Making the dough is simple, and the basic recipe only requires the additional step of deep-frying. A homemade doughnut is bound to impress even the most hardcore diner connoisseur.

The muffin and coffee cake recipes in this chapter are also simple and taste much better than anything made from a commercial mix. The pastry recipes are slightly more time-consuming, but the results are well worth the extra effort. Serve any of these dunkables for breakfast or as an afternoon snack. Or make up a batch of one of them to bring along on a road trip. You can still stop at a diner for the coffee.

Banana-Nut Muffins

1³/₄ cups all-purpose flour

¹/₂ cup unprocessed wheat bran
(not bran cereal)

2 teaspoons baking powder

1 teaspoon ground cinnamon

¹/₂ teaspoon baking soda

¹/₄ teaspoon salt

¹/₈ teaspoon freshly grated nutmeg

³/₄ cup coarsely chopped walnuts

1 large egg

1 cup mashed ripe banana (about
2 large bananas)

³/₄ cup firmly packed light brown sugar

6 tablespoons unsalted butter, melted
and warm

¹/₂ cup sour cream

2 teaspoons vanilla extract

1 teaspoon grated lemon zest

These rustic muffins, fragrant with banana and toasted walnuts, are just the sort of breakfast snack a good, old-fashioned diner serves. Made with a combination of flour and wheat bran, they have a nutty texture and flavor. Sour cream and butter make them extra moist. To ensure tender muffins, don't overmix the batter.

1. Preheat the oven to 350°F. Grease a standard 12-cup muffin pan or line it with paper liners.

2. In a medium bowl, stir together the flour, wheat bran, baking powder, cinnamon, baking soda, salt, and nutmeg with a whisk. Stir in the walnuts.

3. In a large bowl, whisk together the egg, banana, brown sugar, melted butter, sour cream, vanilla extract, and lemon zest until well blended. Add the flour mixture and mix with a wooden spoon just until moistened. Do not overmix. Divide the batter evenly among the muffin cups.

4. Bake for 18 to 20 minutes, or until a toothpick inserted into the center of a muffin comes out clean. Cool in the pan on a wire rack for 5 minutes, then carefully turn out onto the rack. Serve warm or cool completely. Store in an airtight container at room temperature for up to 2 days.

$1.39

Jumbo Crumbly Blueberry Muffins

Makes 6 large muffins

CRUMBLE TOPPING

$^1/_2$ cup all-purpose flour

1 teaspoon ground cinnamon

$^1/_2$ cup firmly packed light brown sugar

$^1/_4$ cup ($^1/_2$ stick) unsalted butter, slightly softened and cut into $^1/_2$-inch pieces

BLUEBERRY MUFFINS

1 cup fresh or frozen (unthawed) blueberries

2 cups plus 1 tablespoon all-purpose flour

$^2/_3$ cup granulated sugar

2 teaspoons baking powder

$^1/_4$ teaspoon baking soda

$^1/_2$ teaspoon ground cinnamon

$^1/_4$ teaspoon salt

1 large egg

1 cup buttermilk

1 teaspoon vanilla extract

6 tablespoons ($^3/_4$ stick) unsalted butter, melted and cooled

These oversized muffins, packed with blueberry flavor, are often found under cake keepers on diner counters. They are best made when the berries are in season, June through August, but are still delicious when made with individually quick-frozen berries (not the ones packed in syrup).

1. To make the crumble topping, in a medium bowl, stir together the flour, cinnamon, and brown sugar. Add the butter pieces and stir and mash the mixture with a fork until the topping is crumbly. Set aside.

2. To make the blueberry muffins, preheat the oven to 350°F. Generously butter six 8-ounce jumbo muffin cups. If using fresh blueberries, rinse and thoroughly dry the berries. In a small bowl, toss the fresh or frozen berries with the 1 tablespoon flour.

3. In a large bowl, stir together the 2 cups flour, sugar, baking powder, baking soda, cinnamon, and salt. Make a well in the center.

4. In a medium bowl, whisk together the egg and buttermilk until combined. Whisk in the vanilla and melted butter. Pour the buttermilk mixture into the well. Begin stirring the liquids, gradually drawing the dry ingredients into the well until they are almost, but not quite, combined. Add the blueberries and fold in just to distribute evenly. Do not overmix. Evenly divide the batter among the 6 prepared muffin cups. Evenly divide the crumble topping among the muffins, sprinkling it on top (about $^1/_4$ cup for each muffin).

5. Bake the muffins for 30 to 35 minutes, or until a toothpick inserted into the center of a muffin comes out clean. Cool in the pan on a wire rack for 10 minutes, then carefully turn out onto the rack. Serve warm, or cool completely. Store in an airtight container at room temperature for up to 2 days.

$1.41

Sour Cream–Blueberry Crumb Cake

CRUMB TOPPING

1 cup all-purpose flour

¹/₄ cup granulated sugar

¹/₃ cup firmly packed dark brown sugar

1 teaspoon ground cinnamon

¹/₄ teaspoon salt

7 tablespoons unsalted butter, melted

CAKE

1¹/₂ cups all-purpose flour

1¹/₄ teaspoons baking powder

¹/₄ teaspoon baking soda

¹/₄ teaspoon salt

1 cup blueberries

1 cup sour cream

1¹/₂ teaspoons vanilla extract

¹/₂ cup plus 2 tablespoons (1¹/₄ sticks) unsalted butter, softened

1 cup granulated sugar

2 large eggs

A crumb cake is a coffee cake that makes a mess when you eat it. Diner menus often feature a plain, peach, or blueberry crumb cake. This cake gets its moistness from sour cream and lots of butter and is full of fresh blueberry flavor. The dark brown sugar gives the crumb topping a buttery caramel flavor.

1. To make the crumb topping, in a medium bowl, stir together the flour, granulated sugar, brown sugar, cinnamon, and salt until well blended. Add the melted butter and mix with a fork, stirring until the butter is absorbed and the dry ingredients are uniformly moistened. Set aside the crumb mixture.

2. To make the cake, preheat the oven to 350°F. Butter and flour a 9-inch square baking pan.

3. In a medium bowl, whisk together the flour, baking powder, baking soda, and salt until well blended; set aside.

4. In a medium bowl, toss the blueberries with 1 tablespoon of the flour mixture until the berries are coated; set aside. In a small bowl, whisk together the sour cream and vanilla extract; set aside.

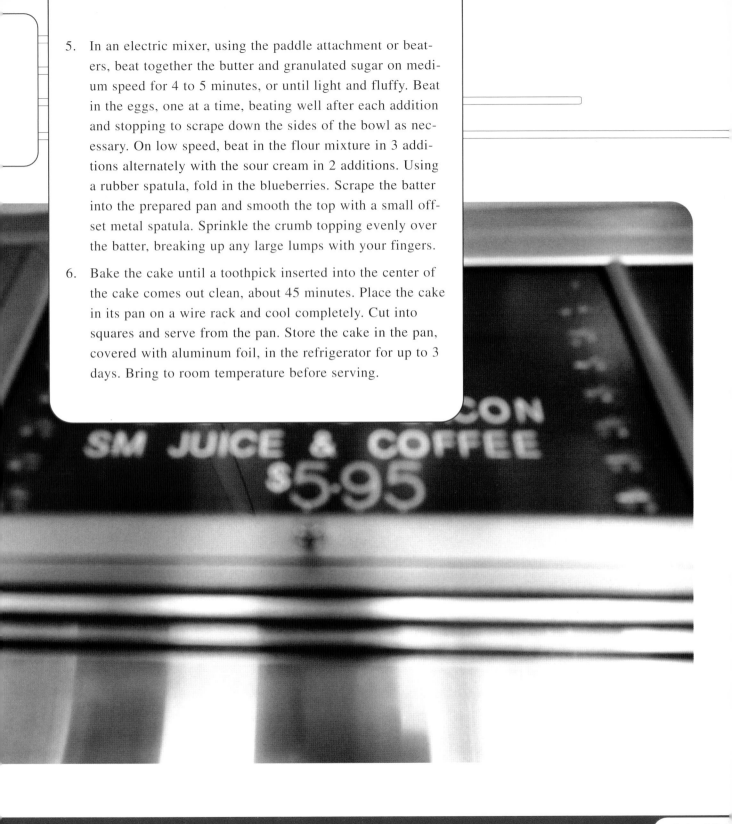

5. In an electric mixer, using the paddle attachment or beaters, beat together the butter and granulated sugar on medium speed for 4 to 5 minutes, or until light and fluffy. Beat in the eggs, one at a time, beating well after each addition and stopping to scrape down the sides of the bowl as necessary. On low speed, beat in the flour mixture in 3 additions alternately with the sour cream in 2 additions. Using a rubber spatula, fold in the blueberries. Scrape the batter into the prepared pan and smooth the top with a small offset metal spatula. Sprinkle the crumb topping evenly over the batter, breaking up any large lumps with your fingers.

6. Bake the cake until a toothpick inserted into the center of the cake comes out clean, about 45 minutes. Place the cake in its pan on a wire rack and cool completely. Cut into squares and serve from the pan. Store the cake in the pan, covered with aluminum foil, in the refrigerator for up to 3 days. Bring to room temperature before serving.

Apple Turnovers

PASTRY

Basic Flaky Pie Crust (page 30)

APPLE FILLING

$1^1/_8$ pounds Granny Smith apples (about 3 medium), peeled, cored, and sliced $^3/_8$ inch thick

1 teaspoon fresh lemon juice

1 tablespoon frozen apple juice concentrate

2 tablespoons unsalted butter

1 teaspoon grated lemon zest

$^1/_2$ cup firmly packed light brown sugar

$^1/_2$ teaspoon ground cinnamon

Pinch of salt

$^1/_2$ teaspoon vanilla extract

2 teaspoons water

ASSEMBLY

1 egg, lightly beaten

ICING

$^1/_2$ cup confectioners' sugar, sifted

1 tablespoon whole milk

These turnovers have a distinctly unpolished appearance, with apple filling bursting here and there through the pastry. They resemble those you'd find in an old-style rural diner. A sugary icing is drizzled on top, delivering just the right amount of sweetness to the dough. Store the leftover apple juice concentrate in the freezer for glazing pork chops before broiling or for adding to an apple pie to boost the flavor.

1. Make the pie pastry dough as directed and chill for at least 2 hours.

2. To make the apple filling, in a medium bowl, toss together the apple slices, lemon juice, and frozen apple concentrate. In a large skillet, melt the butter over high heat. Add the apple mixture and cook, stirring constantly, for 5 minutes, or until the apples are softened on the outside but still slightly crunchy on the inside. Remove the skillet from the heat and let cool completely.

3. In a medium bowl, combine the cooked apple slices with the lemon zest, brown sugar, cinnamon, salt, vanilla extract, and water, tossing to mix well.

4. Preheat the oven to 400°F. Have 2 baking sheets ready.

5. To assemble the turnovers, divide the pastry dough in half. Divide each half into 5 equal pieces. Lightly flour a work surface. Roll out 1 piece of dough into a rough 6-inch round. Place a $5^1/_2$-inch diameter bowl or plate upside down on the round and, using a paring knife, cut around it to form a perfect round. Place on a baking sheet and repeat with the remaining pieces of dough to form a total of 10

$1.44

rounds. Spoon an equal amount of the apple filling onto one-half of each round, leaving a $1/2$-inch border uncovered along the edge. Don't stuff too full, or you will have trouble forming the turnovers. Brush a little beaten egg around one-half of the edge of each round and fold in half, pressing lightly to seal the edge. Using the tines of a fork, press to seal the edge. Brush the top of each turnover with the beaten egg. Using a small, sharp knife, cut 3 small steam vents on the top of each turnover.

6. Bake the turnovers for 20 to 25 minutes, or until the filling is bubbling through the steam vents and the pastry is golden. Transfer to a wire rack and let cool while you prepare the icing.

7. To make the icing, in a medium bowl, whisk together the confectioners' sugar and milk until smooth. Spoon the icing over the warm turnovers, covering the tops. Serve warm or at room temperature. Store in an airtight container in the refrigerator for up to 3 days. Bring to room temperature before serving.

$1.45

Glazed Almond-Cinnamon Swirls

DOUGH

$^1/_2$ cup plus 1 tablespoon warm whole
milk (105° to 110°F)

2 tablespoons granulated sugar

2 teaspoons active dry yeast

2 cups bread flour

$^3/_4$ teaspoon ground cardamom

$^1/_2$ teaspoon salt

1 large egg

$^1/_4$ cup ($^1/_2$ stick) unsalted butter,
softened

ALMOND-CINNAMON FILLING

5 tablespoons granulated sugar

2 teaspoons ground cinnamon

3 tablespoons unsalted butter, softened

$^1/_2$ cup almond paste

$^1/_3$ cup blanched hazelnuts or almonds,
finely ground

1 large egg

2 teaspoons all-purpose flour

$^1/_2$ teaspoon vanilla extract

$^1/_4$ teaspoon almond extract

TOPPING

1 large egg lightly beaten with 1
tablespoon water

$^1/_4$ cup sliced almonds

$^1/_2$ cup confectioners' sugar

1 tablespoon water

This breakfast sweet is in the spirit of the classic diner Danish. Whether in the city or the suburbs, commuters regularly stop off at a diner for a morning sweet to enjoy with their coffee. Made with a butter-enriched bread dough, these snail-shaped pastries are filled with a cinnamon-almond mixture, then sprinkled liberally with sliced almonds and brushed with a sweet icing. Serve them slightly warm.

1. To make the dough, in a small bowl, combine the warm milk with 1 teaspoon of the sugar. Stir the yeast into the mixture and let stand for 10 minutes, or until foamy.

2. In an electric mixer, using the paddle attachment or beaters, combine the flour, the remaining 5 teaspoons sugar, the cardamom, and the salt on low speed. Add the egg and the yeast mixture and continue to mix on low speed until blended. Increase the speed to medium and beat in the butter, 1 tablespoon at a time; continue to beat for about 1 minute. The dough will be smooth but sticky. Switch to the dough hook attachment and mix on medium-low speed for 6 minutes, or until the dough is relatively smooth and elastic. (Alternatively, you may knead the dough by hand on a lightly floured surface for 10 to 15 minutes.) Cover the bowl with plastic wrap and let the dough rest in a warm, draft-free place for 30 minutes, or until doubled in volume.

3. To make the almond-cinnamon filling, in a small bowl, combine 3 tablespoons of the sugar with the cinnamon; set aside.

4. In an electric mixer, using the paddle attachment or beaters, beat the butter on low speed until smooth. Gradually beat in the almond paste and the remaining 2 tablespoons sugar, beating until smooth. Mix in the hazelnuts or almonds, the egg, flour, and vanilla and almond extracts.

5. To assemble the swirls, butter an insulated baking sheet (or use 2 regular baking sheets, stacked one on top of the other). On a lightly floured work surface, roll out the dough into a 14-by-16-inch rectangle. Spread the almond-cinnamon filling over the rectangle. Sprinkle the filling evenly with the cinnamon-sugar mixture. Starting from a long end, roll the dough up into a tight log. Trim off and discard $1/2$ inch from each open end. Cut the log into 14 equal slices, each about $3/4$ inch thick. Place the slices, cut sides down, on the buttered baking sheet. Let the pastries stand at room temperature for 1 hour, or until just about doubled in size.

6. Preheat the oven to 375°F. Tuck the end of each swirl underneath it, so that it will not unravel while baking. Brush the tops of the swirls with the egg-water mixture. Sprinkle with the sliced almonds. Bake the swirls for 20 to 25 minutes, or until golden brown.

7. While the pastries are baking, in a small bowl, whisk together the confectioners' sugar and water until smooth. As soon as the pastries are removed from the oven, brush the sugar mixture over them. Serve the swirls warm or at room temperature. Store in an airtight container in the refrigerator for up to 3 days. Bring to room temperature before serving.

Raspberry Twists

Makes 16 twists

PASTRY DOUGH

$^3/_4$ cup warm whole milk (105° to 110°F)

$^1/_3$ cup granulated sugar

2 teaspoons active dry yeast

$^1/_2$ teaspoon salt

1 egg, lightly beaten

2 tablespoons unsalted butter, melted

$1^1/_2$ teaspoons vanilla extract

$^1/_2$ teaspoon grated lemon zest

$2^3/_4$ cups all-purpose flour

RASPBERRY-ALMOND FILLING

1 cup granulated sugar

1 teaspoon ground cinnamon

1 cup sliced almonds

$^2/_3$ cup seedless raspberry preserves

ASSEMBLY

$^1/_2$ cup (1 stick) unsalted butter, melted

These diner-style pastries are perfect for breakfast, brunch, or a midafternoon coffee break. The raspberry-filled twists are baked so they form a solid golden layer of fragrant pastry, and then are pulled apart and eaten individually. Make sure to use good-quality raspberry preserves—it makes a big difference.

1. To make the pastry dough, in a large mixing bowl, combine the warm milk and sugar. Stir the yeast into the milk mixture and let stand for 10 minutes, or until foamy.

2. Whisk the salt, egg, butter, vanilla, and lemon zest into the milk mixture. Stir in $2^1/_2$ cups of the flour, mixing until the dough holds together. Transfer the dough to a lightly floured work surface and knead until smooth and elastic, adding some or all of the remaining $^1/_4$ cup flour if the dough is too sticky. Shape the dough into a ball and transfer to a buttered bowl. Cover the bowl with plastic wrap and let the dough rise in a warm, draft-free place for about an hour, or until it has doubled in bulk.

3. Butter the bottom and sides of a $17^1/_2$-by-$11^1/_2$-inch jelly-roll pan. In a medium bowl stir together the sugar, cinnamon, and almonds.

4. Punch down the dough and divide it in half. On a lightly floured work surface, roll out 1 piece of the dough into a 9-by-16-inch rectangle. Spread the rectangle with $^1/_3$ cup of the raspberry preserves. Sprinkle evenly with $^1/_4$ cup of the cinnamon-sugar-nut mixture. Carefully pick up a short end and fold the rectangle in half. Press the two surfaces

together. Using a large, sharp knife or pizza wheel, cut the dough lengthwise into 8 strips. Repeat with the remaining dough.

5. To assemble the twists, place the melted butter in a pie pan or other shallow pan. Place the remaining cinnamon-sugar-nut mixture on a plate. Pick up each strip and twist it about 4 times, pulling slightly to elongate it. Place in the melted butter and turn to coat completely. Place in the plate of cinnamon-sugar, again turning to coat. Place the twists side by side in the prepared jelly-roll pan, filling it completely. Cover with plastic wrap and let rise in a warm, draft-free place until almost doubled in bulk, about 45 minutes.

6. Preheat the oven to 375°F. Remove the plastic wrap and bake the twists for 15 to 20 minutes, or until puffed and golden brown. Serve the twists warm or at room temperature, pulling off each individual twist. Store in the covered pan in the refrigerator for up to 3 days.

$1.49

Diner-Style Powdered Buttermilk Doughnuts

Makes 10 doughnuts and about 16 doughnut holes

$3^{1}/_{2}$ cups cake flour

1 teaspoon baking powder

$^{1}/_{4}$ teaspoon baking soda

$1^{1}/_{2}$ teaspoons salt

$^{3}/_{4}$ teaspoon ground cinnamon

$^{1}/_{4}$ teaspoon freshly grated nutmeg

$^{3}/_{4}$ cup granulated sugar

$^{3}/_{4}$ cup buttermilk

3 tablespoons unsalted butter, melted and cooled

1 large egg, at room temperature

2 teaspoons vanilla extract

Vegetable oil for frying

1 cup confectioners' sugar, sifted

Doughnuts were first brought to America by Dutch settlers in New York and have long been a diner counter staple. This version is the classic confectioners' sugar–coated variety, perfect for dunking. The doughnuts should be cooled completely before coating, but they should be served the same day they are made.

1. In a medium bowl, sift together the flour, baking powder, baking soda, salt, cinnamon, and nutmeg. Add the sugar and stir the dry ingredients with a whisk until combined.

2. In a medium bowl, whisk together the buttermilk, melted butter, egg, and vanilla until blended. Make a well in the center of the flour mixture and pour the buttermilk mixture into it. Using a rubber spatula, stir until the mixture forms a soft, moist dough. Dust a work surface with flour. Scrape the dough onto the work surface and lightly sprinkle the top of the dough with flour. Gather the dough into a ball and knead it gently 5 or 6 times, or until smooth. Roll or pat the dough into a round roughly 10 inches in diameter and $^{1}/_{2}$ inch thick. Transfer the round to a baking sheet, cover it with plastic wrap, and place it in the freezer for 15 minutes, or until firm.

3. Using a 3-inch doughnut cutter (or a 3-inch round biscuit cutter and a $^{3}/_{4}$-inch cutter or pastry tip for the hole), cut out 7 doughnuts and holes from the dough. Gather the scraps together, reroll $^{1}/_{2}$ inch thick, and cut out 3 more doughnuts and as many holes as possible. Place the doughnuts and holes on a baking sheet or 2 plates, cover with plastic wrap, and refrigerate while heating the oil for frying.

$1.50

4. Pour the oil into a deep-fat fryer or large straight-sided saucepan to a depth of 2 to 3 inches. Heat the oil to 370°F. Line a baking sheet with paper towels.

5. Fry the doughnuts and holes in small batches, turning once, for 2 to 3 minutes, or until golden brown. Using a slotted spoon, transfer to the paper towels to drain, then place on a wire rack to cool completely.

6. When the doughnuts and holes are completely cool, place the confectioners' sugar in a medium bowl. Generously dredge the doughnuts and holes in the sugar, shaking off the excess. Serve the same day.

Boston Cream Doughnuts

VANILLA CREAM FILLING

$^2/_3$ cup granulated sugar

2 cups whole milk, divided

$^1/_2$ vanilla bean, split lengthwise

$^1/_4$ cup cornstarch

5 large egg yolks

3 tablespoons unsalted butter, softened

DOUGHNUTS

$^3/_4$ cup warm (105° to 110°F) whole milk

$2^1/_4$ teaspoons (1 envelope) active
   dry yeast

$^1/_3$ cup granulated sugar

$2^3/_4$ cups unbleached all-purpose flour

$^1/_4$ teaspoon ground cardamom

$^1/_4$ teaspoon freshly grated nutmeg

1 teaspoon salt

4 large egg yolks

$^1/_2$ cup (1 stick) unsalted butter, cut into
   tablespoons, softened

Vegetable oil for frying

CHOCOLATE GLAZE

4 ounces bittersweet chocolate, finely
   chopped

3 tablespoons water

2 tablespoons light corn syrup

$^1/_3$ cup granulated sugar

3 tablespoons unsalted butter, softened

These doughnuts require a little time to make, but they are far better than anything you'll find in any doughnut shop. The recipe was created by Carole Harlam, a talented baker, dessert maker, and perfectionist. It was inspired by a drive through New England, where she and her family frequently stopped at roadside diners for glazed doughnuts and coffee. Make sure your oil is properly preheated before frying the doughnuts. When it is at the right temperature, the surface will quiver slightly.

1. To make the vanilla cream filling, in a saucepan, combine the sugar, $1^1/_2$ cups of the milk, and the vanilla bean. Cook over low heat, stirring constantly with a wooden spoon, until the sugar is dissolved. Raise the heat and scald the mixture.

2. Meanwhile, place the cornstarch in a medium bowl. Using a wire whisk, gradually whisk in the remaining $^1/_2$ cup milk until smooth. Add the egg yolks and whisk until well blended.

3. Slowly pour $^1/_3$ cup of the hot milk mixture into the yolk mixture, whisking constantly. Gradually whisk in the rest of the hot milk. Return the milk-yolk mixture to the saucepan and bring to a boil over medium heat. Boil gently for 1 minute, stirring constantly.

4. Remove the pan from the heat and whisk in the butter. Pass the mixture through a fine-mesh sieve into a bowl. Cover with plastic wrap, pressing it directly onto the surface, and refrigerate until chilled.

5. To make the doughnuts, place the warm milk, yeast, and 1 teaspoon of the sugar in the bowl of an electric mixer. Stir the yeast into the mixture and let stand for 10 minutes, or until foamy.

6. Add 1 cup of the flour and, using the paddle attachment or beaters, beat on low speed for 2 minutes to form the sponge. Remove the bowl from the stand, cover with plastic wrap, and let the sponge stand at room temperature until well risen, about 30 minutes.

7. In a medium bowl, whisk together the remaining $1^3/_4$ cups flour with the cardamom, nutmeg, and salt; set aside.

8. Return the bowl containing the sponge to the mixer stand. Using the paddle attachment on medium speed, add the egg yolks and mix until incorporated, then beat in the remaining sugar. Add the butter, 1 tablespoon at a time, beating until each tablespoon is absorbed before adding the next. Add the flour-spice mixture and beat on medium speed for 5 minutes. The dough will not form a ball. It will be soft and part of it will wrap itself around the paddle.

9. Scrape the dough into a well-buttered bowl and turn as needed to coat all sides with the butter. Cover the bowl with buttered plastic wrap, buttered side down, and let the dough rise in a warm, draft-free place for about 1 hour, or until it has slightly more than doubled in volume.

10. Turn out the dough onto a lightly oiled work surface. Using your hands, gently press down on it to deflate it and flatten it evenly to no less then $1/_2$ inch thick. Cover loosely with plastic wrap and let the dough rest for 5 minutes.

11. Line a baking sheet with parchment or waxed paper. Using a floured $2^1/_2$-inch biscuit cutter, cut out 14 dough rounds. Gently transfer the rounds to the lined baking sheet, reshaping them if necessary. Space the rounds at least 1 inch apart to allow for expansion. Let rise for about 30 minutes, or until almost doubled in size.

RECIPE CONTINUES >>

12. While the doughnuts are rising, pour the oil into a deep-fat fryer or large straight-sided saucepan to a depth of 2 to 3 inches. Heat the oil to 360°F. Line a baking sheet with paper towels.

13. Fry the doughnuts, 3 or 4 at a time, for about 1 minute, or until golden brown on the first side. Turn and fry on the second side until golden brown. It may take slightly less time for the second side to cook than the first. The midline of the doughnut will be lighter than the rest of it, which is characteristic. Using a slotted spoon, transfer the doughnuts to the paper towels to drain, then place on a wire rack to cool. As soon as the doughnuts are cool enough to handle, use a long, thin, plain pastry tip to poke a hole through the midline to the center of each doughnut. Let cool completely before filling.

14. Remove the vanilla cream filling from the refrigerator and beat with the electric mixer on medium speed until smooth.

15. Scrape the cream filling into a large pastry bag fitted with a medium plain tip (such as Ateco #2). Pipe the filling into the hole in the middle of each doughnut until the doughnut feels full. Wipe off any excess cream. Return the filled doughnuts to the rack as they are filled.

16. To make the chocolate glaze, place the chopped chocolate in a medium heatproof bowl. Set aside.

17. Combine the water, corn syrup, and sugar in a heavy-bottomed, medium saucepan. Place over low heat and cook, stirring constantly with a wooden spoon, until the sugar is dissolved. Raise the heat and bring to a full boil.

18. Pour the hot syrup over the chopped chocolate. Let stand for 3 minutes to melt the chocolate, then whisk gently until smooth. Whisk in the butter. Let the glaze cool until it starts to thicken slightly, stirring occasionally.

19. Spread a scant tablespoon of chocolate glaze over the top of each doughnut. Place the glazed doughnuts back on the rack and let stand until set. The doughnuts are best served within a few hours.

CHAPTER 11

From the Soda Fountain

The excited whir of a heavy-duty shake blender, the whoosh of a whipped cream nozzle: these are familiar diner sounds. Soda-fountain drinks and desserts, once served predominantly at drugstore counters, are now standard offerings at the diner counter. It was not so long ago that the diner was a traditional Saturday-night destination for couples sharing ice cream sodas, or a place where children were rewarded for good behavior with ice cream sundaes. But today, you can still rest your arms on the cool Formica counter at a diner and order outrageously voluptuous ice cream desserts.

This chapter features the most popular of these soda fountain favorites, from an old-style root beer float to a hot fudge sundae to an extravagant banana split. I promise that my fountain recipes will not disillusion those who, after consuming a diner sundae or shake, sometimes feel a sense of disappointment–that the serving glass was too small, or that the sauce, likely made with artificial ingredients, was poured from an industrial-sized container. And all are easy to make, requiring, after the sauces or syrups are made, simple assembly and a hunger for a big, old-fashioned ice-cold dessert. And don't hold the cherry.

Root Beer Float

2 cans or bottles (12 ounces each) root
   beer, chilled

2 scoops vanilla ice cream

The key to this popular beverage-dessert is the root beer, not the ice cream. Not all root beers are created equal. The world's two leading soft-drink companies market their own mediocre brands, while aggressively elbowing aside the competition (which usually has better-tasting products). Here are my recommendations from among the root beer survivors, if you can get them: Hires, Stewart's, and Boylan's. As for the ice cream, I wouldn't bother with the expensive premium brands. Practically any decent vanilla will do.

1. Place two tall, 18-ounce glasses in the freezer for at least 30 minutes, or until ice-cold.

2. Pour the root beer into the iced glasses, filling them three-fourths full (including the head). Top each with a scoop of vanilla ice cream and serve immediately with a straw and a long spoon.

Makes 2 servings

Doubly dark, this shake gets a chocolate lift from a homemade semisweet chocolate syrup and chocolate ice cream. For extra indulgence, float a scoop of chocolate ice cream on top and serve with a straw and a long spoon.

1. Place two tall, 18-ounce glasses in the freezer for at least 30 minutes, or until ice-cold.

2. To make the chocolate syrup, place the chocolate in a small heatproof bowl. In a small saucepan, heat the milk just until it begins to boil. Remove the pan from the heat and pour the hot milk over the chocolate. Let the mixture stand for 1 minute, then whisk until completely smooth.

3. Place the bowl of syrup into a larger bowl of ice water. Stir until cold, about 5 minutes. Remove the bowl from the ice water.

4. To make the milk shake, in a blender, combine the milk and 1 scoop of the ice cream. Blend on high speed for about 20 seconds, or until smooth. With the motor running, add the chocolate syrup and the remaining scoop of ice cream and blend until smooth.

5. Divide the shake evenly between the chilled glasses and serve immediately with straws.

CHOCOLATE SYRUP

2 ounces semisweet chocolate, finely chopped

$1/2$ cup whole milk

MILK SHAKE

1 cup whole milk

2 large scoops chocolate ice cream

$1.59

Butterscotch Sundae

BUTTERSCOTCH SAUCE

5 tablespoons unsalted butter, cut into tablespoons

3/4 cup firmly packed light brown sugar

1/2 cup light corn syrup

1/2 cup heavy cream

3/4 teaspoon salt

1 teaspoon vanilla extract

ASSEMBLY

1 1/2 pints vanilla ice cream

1/4 cup chopped walnuts (optional)

Sweetened whipped cream

4 maraschino cherries

Although ice cream of any flavor can be used in a sundae, vanilla ice cream and butterscotch sauce are particularly well suited to each other. The butterscotch sauce is easy to make and is far better than most bottled varieties. The amount of salt in the recipe may seem high, but it balances the sweetness of the brown sugar.

1. To make the butterscotch sauce, in a medium saucepan, combine the butter, brown sugar, corn syrup, cream, and salt. Place over medium-high heat and cook, stirring occasionally, until the mixture comes to a boil. Let the mixture boil, without stirring, for 2 minutes. Remove the pan from the heat and cool for 15 minutes, whisking occasionally. Stir in the vanilla. Transfer the sauce to a glass measuring cup. Cover loosely with plastic wrap and cool completely. (The sauce may be stored in an airtight container in the refrigerator for up to 5 days.)

2. To assemble the sundaes, place about 1 tablespoon of the cooled butterscotch sauce in the bottom of each of 4 sundae glasses. Place a medium scoop of the ice cream in each glass. Top with a generous drizzle of butterscotch sauce, a sprinkle of nuts (if using), and then another scoop of ice cream. Drizzle more sauce onto the sundaes, add another sprinkling of nuts, and top each with a generous dollop of whipped cream and a maraschino cherry. Serve immediately.

Hot Fudge Walnut Sundae

WARM WALNUT SAUCE

1 cup granulated sugar

$^1/_3$ cup water

1 teaspoon fresh lemon juice

$^1/_2$ cup walnut pieces

$^1/_2$ cup heavy cream

HOT FUDGE SAUCE

3 ounces semisweet chocolate, chopped

2 tablespoons unsalted butter

$^3/_4$ cup heavy cream

$^1/_4$ cup light corn syrup

$^1/_2$ cup granulated sugar

2 teaspoons vanilla extract

WHIPPED CREAM

1 cup heavy cream

2 tablespoons granulated sugar

1 teaspoon vanilla extract

ASSEMBLY

4 scoops vanilla ice cream (or the
   ice cream of your choice)

1 tablespoon finely chopped walnuts

2 maraschino cherries

In the nineteenth century, soda drinks were considered to be an indulgence and their sale was prohibited on Sunday. In the 1880s, to bypass this ordinance, soda shops began serving soda-less "sundaes," which consisted of ice cream, syrup, and whipped cream. This sundae is a contrast in textures and temperatures. It combines cold, creamy vanilla ice cream with warm, crunchy walnut sauce and rich hot fudge sauce. Extra hot fudge sauce is served on the side, so you won't run out.

1. To make the warm walnut sauce, in a medium, heavy saucepan, combine the sugar, water, and lemon juice and cook over medium heat, stirring constantly, until the sugar dissolves. Increase the heat to medium-high, stop stirring, and cook the mixture until it turns golden brown. Immediately add the walnuts and cook, stirring constantly, for about 1 minute, or until the nuts are lightly toasted. Remove the pan from the heat and carefully stir in the cream, $^1/_4$ cup at a time. Return the pan to medium heat and cook, stirring constantly, just until the sauce is well blended. Keep warm.

2. To make the hot fudge sauce, in a medium saucepan, combine the chocolate, butter, and cream. Place over medium heat, stirring, until the chocolate is completely melted. Add the corn syrup and sugar and cook, stirring constantly, until the sauce just begins to simmer. Reduce the heat and simmer gently, without stirring, for 15 minutes, or until thickened.

3. Remove the pan from the heat and stir in the vanilla extract. Use the sauce immediately or reheat in a double boiler or in a microwave before serving.

4. To make the whipped cream, in an electric mixer, using the whisk attachment or beaters, beat the heavy cream on medium-low speed for 30 seconds. Increase the speed to medium-high and add the sugar and vanilla. Beat until the cream forms soft peaks. Scrape the cream into a pastry bag fitted with a large star tip (such as Ateco #8) and refrigerate until ready to assemble the sundaes.

5. To assemble the sundaes, pour some of the warm walnut sauce into the bottom of a sundae glass. Top with a scoop of ice cream, a generous spoonful of hot fudge sauce, another scoop of ice cream, and a spoonful of each sauce. Top with a dramatic swirl of whipped cream. Sprinkle with the finely chopped walnuts and top with a maraschino cherry. Repeat to make another sundae. Serve each sundae with a small pitcher or bowl of extra hot fudge sauce on the side.

$1.63

S'more Sundae

GRAHAM CRACKER PEANUT LAYER

6 whole graham crackers, coarsely broken

1/4 cup unsalted roasted peanuts

1 tablespoon granulated sugar

3 tablespoons unsalted butter, melted

WHIPPED CREAM

1 cup heavy cream

2 tablespoons sugar

ASSEMBLY

1 cup marshmallow spread such as Marshmallow Fluff

1 cup Chocolate Sauce (page 166)

8 scoops vanilla fudge swirl or rocky road ice cream

GARNISH

1/4 cup coarsely chopped unsalted roasted peanuts

4 maraschino cherries

Named because they're so good you'll always want "some more," s'mores are the union of toasted marshmallow and chocolate, sandwiched between graham crackers. This sundae was inspired by the ubiquitous campfire treat and combines vanilla fudge swirl ice cream with marshmallow, chocolate sauce, whipped cream, and peanut-studded graham cracker pieces. Who needs to go camping to have a great time?

1. To make the graham cracker peanut layer, preheat the oven to 350°F. Butter the bottom of a 9-inch pie pan. Place the graham crackers in a food processor and process until finely ground. Add the peanuts and sugar and process until the peanuts are finely chopped. Stir in the melted butter until combined.

2. Transfer the crumb mixture to the prepared pie pan and, using your fingers, press it evenly onto the bottom of the pan. Bake for 15 minutes, or until the crust is set and is just beginning to brown. Place the pan on a wire rack and cool completely.

3. Using a small knife or your fingers, break the crust up into uneven pieces, each about 1 inch square. Set the pieces aside until ready to assemble the sundaes.

4. To make the whipped cream, in an electric mixer, using the whisk attachment or beaters, beat the cream on medium-low speed for 30 seconds. Increase the speed to medium-high and add the sugar. Beat until the cream forms soft peaks. Scrape the whipped cream into a pastry bag fitted with a medium star tip (such as Ateco #6) and refrigerate the bag until ready to assemble the desserts.

$1.64

CHAPTER 11: FROM THE SODA FOUNTAIN

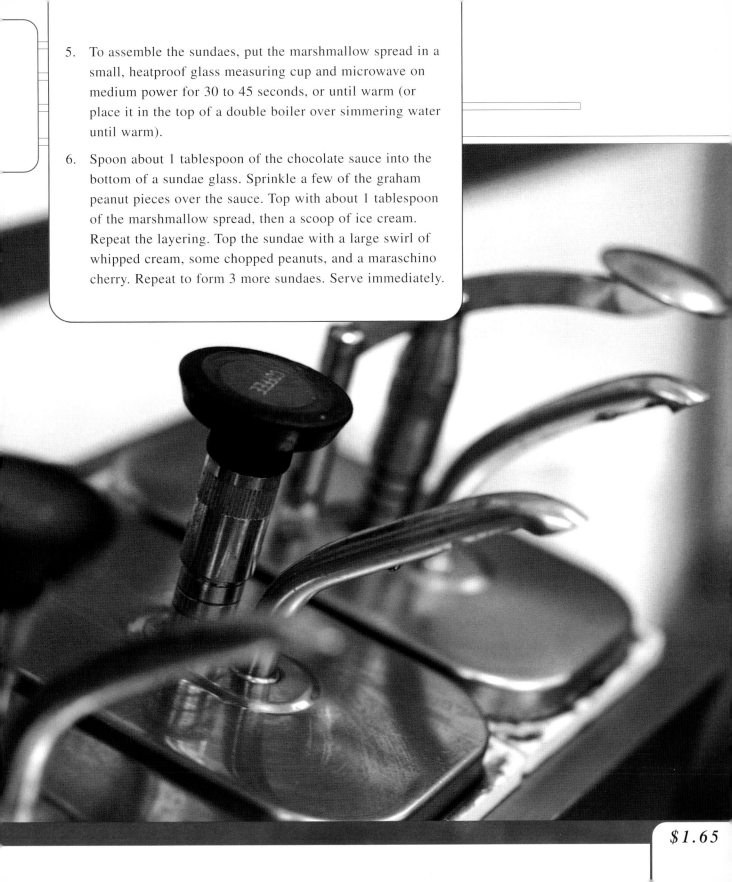

5. To assemble the sundaes, put the marshmallow spread in a small, heatproof glass measuring cup and microwave on medium power for 30 to 45 seconds, or until warm (or place it in the top of a double boiler over simmering water until warm).

6. Spoon about 1 tablespoon of the chocolate sauce into the bottom of a sundae glass. Sprinkle a few of the graham peanut pieces over the sauce. Top with about 1 tablespoon of the marshmallow spread, then a scoop of ice cream. Repeat the layering. Top the sundae with a large swirl of whipped cream, some chopped peanuts, and a maraschino cherry. Repeat to form 3 more sundaes. Serve immediately.

$1.65

Triple-Threat Banana Split

STRAWBERRY SAUCE

6 strawberries, hulled

2 tablespoons fresh orange juice

1 tablespoon granulated sugar

CHOCOLATE SAUCE

2 tablespoons unsalted butter

2 tablespoons whole milk

2 tablespoons heavy cream

1 tablespoon granulated sugar

2 ounces semisweet chocolate, chopped

2 ounces milk chocolate, chopped

WHIPPED CREAM

³/₄ cup heavy cream

2 tablespoons granulated sugar

ASSEMBLY

1 large, ripe banana

1 scoop each vanilla, chocolate, and
   strawberry ice cream

¹/₄ cup Butterscotch Sauce (page 160)

¹/₄ cup chopped walnuts

2 maraschino cherries

This is the ultimate ice cream sundae. With three ice creams, three luscious sauces, mounds of sweetened whipped cream, chopped walnuts, and two cherries to tip the scale, it is the supreme dessert celebration. A banana split made with home-made sauces will dazzle even the most jaded diner-counter groupie.

1. To make the strawberry sauce, put the strawberries, orange juice, and sugar in a food processor and pulse until the berries are coarsely chopped. Transfer to a small bowl or measuring cup, cover, and refrigerate until ready to assemble the dessert.

2. To make the chocolate sauce, in a small saucepan, combine the butter, milk, heavy cream, and sugar. Place over medium heat and bring to a gentle boil. Reduce the heat to low and add both chocolates. Cook, stirring constantly, until the chocolates are completely melted and the sauce is smooth. Remove from heat.

3. To make the whipped cream, in an electric mixer, using the whisk attachment or beaters, beat the cream on medium-low speed for 30 seconds. Increase the speed to medium-high and add the sugar. Beat until the cream forms soft peaks. Scrape the whipped cream into a pastry bag fitted with a large star tip (Ateco #8) and refrigerate until ready to assemble the dessert.

$1.66

4. To assemble the split, peel the banana and cut it in half lengthwise. Arrange the 3 scoops of ice cream in a banana split dish. Lay a banana half on each side of the ice cream. Pour about $1/4$ cup of the chocolate sauce over the chocolate ice cream. Spoon a generous amount of the strawberry sauce over the strawberry ice cream. Pour the butterscotch sauce over the vanilla ice cream. Sprinkle half of the chopped nuts evenly over the 3 scoops of ice cream. Pipe the whipped cream in dramatic swirls over the dessert. Garnish with the remaining nuts and the maraschino cherries.

Diner Slang

Adam's ale: plain water

A-pie: apple pie

Axle grease: butter

Blonde and sweet: coffee with sugar and cream

Bottom: scoop of ice cream added to a drink

Bucket of cold mud: bowl of chocolate ice cream

Bucket of hail: glass of ice

Burn it and let it swim: chocolate float

Burn one all the way: chocolate milk shake with chocolate ice cream

Chopper: table knife

City juice: water

Coffee and: coffee and a doughnut

Cold spot: iced tea

Cup of mud: coffee

Draw one: coffee

Echo: repeat the order

Eighty-one: glass of water

Eighty-six: all out of a menu item

Eve with a lid on: apple pie

Fifty-five: a glass of root beer

Fifty-one: hot chocolate

Five: glass of milk

Fluff it: add whipped cream

Forty-one: lemonade

George Eddy: customer who doesn't leave a tip

Go for a walk: take-out order

Gravel train: sugar bowl

Graveyard stew: milk toast

Hold the hail: no ice

Hops: malted milk powder

Houseboat: banana split

Ice the rice: add ice cream to rice pudding

In the hay: strawberry milk shake

Java: coffee

Jerk: ice cream soda

Joe: coffee

L.A.: add a scoop of ice cream

Life preservers with a hot top: doughnuts with hot chocolate

Mama: marmalade

Mike and Ike: salt and pepper

Mud: black coffee with chocolate syrup

Nervous pudding: Jell-O

No cow: hold the milk

Oil: butter

P.C.: plain chocolate milk

Pair of drawers: two cups of coffee

Pipes: straws

P.T.: pot of tea

Sand: sugar

Sea dust: salt

Shoot one from the south: make a strong cola

Sinkers and suds: doughnuts and coffee

Squeeze one: orange juice

Twenty-one: limeade

Velvet: a milk shake

Yum-yum: sugar

Suggestions for Further Reading

Books

Clark, Marian. *The Route 66 Cookbook.*
Tulsa: Council Oak Books, 1993.

————. *The Main Street of America Cookbook: A Culinary Journey Down Route 66.*
Tulsa and San Francisco: Council Oak Books, 1997.

Gutman, Richard J. S., and Elliott Kaufman. *American Diner.*
New York, Hagerstown, San Francisco, London: Harper & Row, 1979.

Heiman, Jim. *Car Hops and Curb Service: A History of American Drive-In Restaurants, 1920–1960.*
San Francisco: Chronicle Books, 1996.

McLeod, Elizabeth, and Linda Everett. *Blue Plate Special: The American Diner Cookbook.*
Nashville: Cumberland House Publishing, 1996.

Offitzer, Karen. *Diners.*
New York: MetroBooks, 1997.

Sax, Richard. *Classic Home Desserts: A Treasury of Heirloom and Contemporary Recipes from Around the World.*
Shelburne, VT: Chapters Publishing Ltd, 1994.

Magazines

Roadside Magazine, including its Web site at http://www.roadsidemagazine.com.

Henderson, Janice Wald. "Diner Desserts," *Chocolatier Magazine,* June 1997.

$1.70

$1.73

Table of Equivalents

The exact equivalents in the following tables have been rounded for convenience.

Liquid/Dry Measures

U.S. = Metric

$1/4$ teaspoon = 1.25 milliliters

$1/2$ teaspoon = 2.5 milliliters

1 teaspoon = 5 milliliters

1 tablespoon (3 teaspoons) =
 15 milliliters

1 fluid ounce (2 tablespoons) =
 30 milliliters

$1/4$ cup = 60 milliliters

$1/3$ cup = 80 milliliters

$1/2$ cup = 120 milliliters

1 cup = 240 milliliters

1 pint (2 cups) = 480 milliliters

1 quart (4 cups, 32 ounces) =
 960 milliliters

1 gallon (4 quarts) = 3.84 liters

1 ounce (by weight) = 28 grams

1 pound = 454 grams

2.2 pounds = 1 kilogram

Length

U.S. = Metric

$1/8$ inch = 3 millimeters

$1/4$ inch = 6 millimeters

$1/2$ inch = 12 millimeters

1 inch = 2.5 centimeters

Oven Temperature

Fahrenheit = Celsius = Gas

250 = 120 = $1/2$

275 = 140 = 1

300 = 150 = 2

325 = 160 = 3

350 = 180 = 4

375 = 190 = 5

400 = 200 = 6

425 = 220 = 7

450 = 230 = 8

475 = 240 = 9

500 = 260 = 10

$1.76